UPWARD CHANGE

UPWARD CHANGE

GERALD MIDDENTS

UPWARD CHANGE

iUniverse books may be ordered through booksellers or by contacting:

iUniverse
1663 Liberty Drive
Bloomington, IN 47403
www.iuniverse.com
844-349-9409

ISBN: 978-1-6632-1486-7 (sc)
ISBN: 978-1-6632-1487-4 (e)

Print information available on the last page.

iUniverse rev. date: 01/15/2021

"*Be the change you want to see in the world!*"

Mahatma Gandhi

CONTENTS

PREFACE

I still recall from many decades ago,

Feedback from my key professor.

His assignment for a presentation

To create a theme for direction.

I turned in a theme on "Change!"

But he rejected it in an exchange!

He criticized change as too broad;

He wanted a purpose to be focused.

But I continued to be determined;

Completing a presentation as tailored.

Yes, my dogged determination paid off;

As it became rated as one of the best!

Yes, "CHANGE" prompts varied responses;

Some are negative and others as positive.

This prompts me to be even more careful

As the title of this book will be hopeful!

Contemporary life is almost overwhelming;

With new changes as inspiring or stifling!

Change is a very dynamic perspective;

Since change can help as a corrective.

But change can be very threatening;

It often requires humans to be adapting!

We may need to shift or replace a pattern;

It could also be very likely to feel threatened.

As change is more than different clothing;

It may require us to do some correcting!

Old habits may now be too limiting;

We may need to do new discovering!

The coronavirus requires making changes!

Wearing a mask to protect in conversations.

We may not be able to pursue our profession;

We may make changes in worship and religion.

Change can also be known as "a conversion!"

This dynamic means switching direction!

Children now have to study differently;

This disease also threatens the elderly!

This book identifies changing dynamics!

So we do not need to get into a panic.

"Hopefully, reading it will be helpful!"

Writing this book required thoroughness!

As we citizens arrive at the year 2021,

We clearly observe change has begun.

The United States has a New President,

Kamala Harris serves with Joe Biden.

Former President has trouble letting go;

Trump's narcissism expressed his ego.

He needed to be the center of attention,

Media fed this need for personal recognition.

Now Global Affairs are in high ferment;

Coronavirus infects too many millions!

Nations need to work together for action,

The Whole Earth searches for union!

Global Warming needs to be addressed;[1]

And decisions now can be practiced.

Migration affects so many persons,

Agreements are essential for union.

We must move from "Meism" to "Weism!"[2]

Jointly, "WE" hope to address the problems.

Humanity needs to now work together

Hoping to make changes for the better!

This book tries to recognize changes,

But it is also aware of having limits.

---

[1] Middents, G., 2020, <u>HEATING the EARTH! GLOBAL WARMING,</u> iUniverse Books, Bloomington, Indiana.

[2] Putnam, R., 2020, <u>THE UPSWING: How American Came Together a Century Ago and How WE Can Do It Again,</u> Simon and Schuster, New York.

Future generations depend upon us;

As their Ancestors, "in us they trust!"

Who is now responsible for tomorrow?

Will our future bring us joy or sorrow?

People of faith look to God as Creator;

Looking ahead to Divine Providence!

We also remember our own Forebears;

Generations bore us as our Progenitors!

They passed to us their own qualities;

We inherited part of their legacies!

We also help our new generations;

Hopefully, we provide good changes!

Of course our contributions have limits

As new generations are "experiments!"

We are hopeful for our posterity!

Hoping they contribute to history.

One cynical person had questions;

These may give you indigestion:

"Why should I be concerned with posterity?"

Plus "What has posterity ever done for me?"

Such skepticism now merits our attention,

Since we are looking at our extinction!
These questions raise our consideration; [3]

Future generations have done nil for me!

They are dependent on our contributions.

So let us develop constructive solutions.

Yes, changes are happening now!

So let us "put our hand to the plow!"

Planting good seeds for the future!

For us to work and also nurture!

---

[3]   Op.cit., 2007, BRIDGING FEAR and PEACE: From Bullying to Doing Justice, Manipal University Press, India.

I. DOMESTICALLY

1. POLITICALLY

Life formed biologically from minerals!
   These elements are known as chemicals!
      In between were more billions of years.
   The universe developed into animals!
After millions of years into humanoids!

Animals developed into distinct species!
   Governed by multiplying into creatures!
      These inherited genes from predecessors!
   As primitives they were governed by size
Largest physically dominated less powerful!

Any type of freedom had many limitations!
   The smaller of a species had oppression!
      Their destiny ruled by crude domination!
   Behavior physically was our determination;
Cannibal practices likely had application!

Females typically were dominated by males!
   A hierarchy controlled almost all females!
      Their offspring emerged into these arenas!
   When strength was lost by alpha males;
Their new conqueror destined to prevail!

If males could not hunt for survival foods
   They were dispensable to be consumed!
      These primitive conditions prevailed!
   Species could readily become devoured!
Genetic-social factors surely dominated!

1

Predecessors of homo-sapiens survived!
They combated animals & cold conditions
Sheer physical endurance then dominated!
Intelligence developed with these ancients;
Gradually emerging into social dominance!

Oppression of women and children prevailed!
Subordinate with exception to older males!
The hunters and gatherers for sustenance!
Evolutionary survival was an inheritance;
Living forward depended on intelligence!

Like other species, these humans struggled
To produce survivors who also struggled!
As conditions did change, many perished
By example, their youngsters learned
To pass on skills that they had earned!

Males prevailed with their domination!
Children were laborers as possessions.
The women engaged in plant production!
No longer nomadic life an only option;
As communities settled into locations!

The poor were attached to the land!
Owners saw them as possessions!
Slavery held many as concessions!
Freedom was restricted on locations
Slaves may be held for expansion!

Safety was secondary to functions;
Serving the will of those owners!
Traded like merchandise for sale!
Security was dependent on value;
Less than human in many venues!

When disposed for lacking in value
   Slaves may become beggars anew!
      Depending upon human sympathy
   Animals and slaves were property;
Surviving on minimum destiny

Exploitation became very typical!
   Using their slaves as raw material!
      Disposed of when no longer vital!
   Animals may be treated better!
Traded as merchandise by seller!

Human value concepts were slim;
   Life was short and outlook dim!
      Size and strength was valuable;
   Plus skills that they were capable!
Their destiny depended upon owners!

SERFS IN SERVITUDE

Serfdom and slavery were similar
   Serfs more attached to agriculture.
      There was very little human virtue!
   They were obedient to be secure;
Freedom limited and few endured!

Inequalities were obviously apparent;
   The workers and wealthy aristocrats!
      Social strata followed strict sequels!
   Royalty ruled while subject served;
Levels of respect were differentiated!

Rural life was then predominant;
   Small villages and cities prominent!

Tribal loyalties were pre -eminent!
Kings had rivals who were enemies
Serfs and slaves became their armies!

Knighthood was a style of chivalry!
Rivals leaders used them readily!
Knights influenced future destiny!
The Royalty decided upon liberty;
Subjects acquiesced their humanity!

Serfs and slaves lead by masters;
Masters were under commanders!
These were guided by royal orders!
Life then had a clear hierarchy;
Everyone was loyal to Monarchy!

FULFILLING MATURITY

Living fully is hopefully facilitated!
Psycho-social-physical appreciated!
Plus spiritual faith for wholeness
For living humans to reach fullness!

Sensitivity to these developments
Is helpful in gender management!
Natural changes occur in species!
By recognizing changes in realities!

Without appreciations, clashes occur!
Informed awareness is preferable!
When better civility is advisable---
By helping people to be capable!

Masculinity is physically expressed;
    Femininity tends to be sensitized!
       Even men can be socially assertive;
         And women tend to be more flexible!

      Masculine aggression leads to trouble!
    Historically masculine wars are global!
  Feminine people are more peaceful!
In finding mutuality as agreeable!

People can learn assertiveness!
  Balancing aggression and passiveness!
    These assertive skills are promising!
      For masculine-feminine peace-building!

    As people develop skills for Human Rights
   With hope for global humanity in sight!
  Exploitation is replaced by social justice;
As humanity practices responsible ethics!

      Masculine aggression leads to trouble!
    Historically masculine wars are global!
  Feminine people are more peaceful!
In finding mutuality as agreeable!

    Women tend to be more flexible;
      Feminine people are more peaceful!
In finding mutuality as agreeable!
Men often engage in being debatable!

People can activate assertiveness!
      Balancing aggression and passiveness!
    These assertive skills are very promising!
   Modeling masculine-feminine peace-building!

As people develop skills for Human Rights
With hope for global humanity in sight!
Exploitation is replaced by social justice
As humanity practices responsible ethics!
Centuries of Variable Leadership
The office Seekers in Democracies,
Who often pursue political processes,
From backgrounds with wide varieties!

Washington, invited by citizens
National crises calls for leadership,
Lincoln felt compelled to make sacrifices.

Theodore Roosevelt had big ego needs,
Who sought to play on the big stage!
W. Wilson had democratic ideologies.

Coolidge and Harding were opaque,
They possessed few leadership skills,
Their legacy demonstrated poverty of vision.

Hoover engineered a deep depression,
His gap in economics beyond recession!
USA needed FDR in the nineteen-thirties!

Matching America with F.D. Roosevelt,
Is interpreted as becoming fortunate!
His timely leadership exhausted his energy.

In WW II Truman was thrust into crises,
Being a reluctant "V-P" with his hesitancy.
Eisenhower had trusted dedication to country.

Kennedy groomed as patriarchal,
He responded to his family heritage!
Johnson served out of his inflated persona!

L.B. Johnson was known as a controller,
        Recognized flamboyant Texas' Senator!
    His energy wore out personal staffers!

The Nixon was our Vice-President,
        Whose own self-image became trickier!
          His paranoia eventually spilled socially!

          Jimmy Carter felt somewhat compelled,
        By his convictions internally held,
    He won an election over Gerald Ford!

Ron Reagan possessed an inflated ego!
        An actor seeking to play a big role!
          His talents did not match Presidential.

George H.W. Bush remains a mystery,
        He adapted himself to be in history!
      Son "w" reacted to Father's weaknesses.

Bill Clinton became ambitious,
        Articulating as a wonk into policy!
          His story is now being interpreted widely!
Moreover, Hillary Clinton is ambitious,
        A pioneering woman possessing visions!
    Her career impact is unfolding currently.

Gore and Bush were very different,
George "W." assumed God called him!
        His image as a decider became a disaster!

Barack Obama served in this office,
        Talented person trying to do is best,
    He inherited the legacy of George W.

In 2012, the U.S. had a water-shed,
*   Republicans for four years as obstinate.*
M. Romney seeks entrepreneurial influence!

Some business executives often assume,
*   That leading government is a business!*
*   This model has limits in global affairs.*

Leadership demands some sacrifices,
*   Lacking in entrepreneurial candidates!*
*   Ambition attracts seeking glorification.*

Political parties may actually degenerate,
*   Serving as promoters of ideologies!*
*   Requirements not selected by parties.*

We need intentional preparation!
*   Grooming and shifting-out light chaff!*
*   For multi-gifted leaders democracy awaits.*

Competencies of very trusted leaders,
*   Have parental empathy as Father-Mothers!*
*   Handling sibling squabbles is fundamental!*

Capacities to choose the advisers,
*   Who complements the gaps of leaders!*
*   Coaching teams on wide global concerns.*

Presidents are keen about communicating,
*   Talents educating the public by teaching,*
*   Experienced leaders cultivate listening!*

The successful leaders need confidence,
*   Changing hats to engage voters & diplomats!*
*   Are multi-talents possible in human beings?*

Cultivating leaders' to be honest,
        Inflated egos tempt them to be divine!
    Energetic enthusiasm still authentic!

2. ECONOMICALLY

Why is our hope so powerful?
        How does hope motivate us?
           Is living without hope plausible?

Hope is not a recent discovery!
        So why is hope so inspirational?
        What are your ideas while reading?

Human experience historically values hope!
        Life is better experienced by great expectations!
           Envisioning future hope requires imagination!

"Without hope, people perish!"
        "Faith, Hope and Love abide!" [4]
    Hope can actually keep us alive!

Hope inspires us to keep on trying!
        Being hopeful can keep organizations vying!
          Prolonged hopelessness becomes draining!

Poverty of hopelessness and unemployment,
        Does tests humans for becoming significant!
    Otherwise we may feel unimportant!

Relationships and purpose keeps us going!
        Remember these verses to be forward looking!
At the end, read this page again to keep on hoping!

---

[4]   The Bible, First Corinthians 13

Human differences are readily apparent!
Both economic disparities and confinement!
Actual living conditions are extremely important!

Constitutions ideally value equality!
Genetic composition is 99.9% similarity!
The other 0.01% illustrates enormous variety!

Being born into poverty is a key factor!
Circumstances are the major determinants!
Families, schools, health and good nutrients!

A single parent is constantly struggling!
Our adequate resources are always limiting.
Food and safety plus unavailable housing!

Children born to wealthy have assets!
Those raised in poverty have liabilities!
A fortunate number learn with abilities!

"Equality" is an ideal cultural myth!
Yes, in God's eyes we all have worth!
While major disparities happen on earth!

Jesus' earthy family was among the poor!
His identity in this world was very insecure!
His teachings valued poor; not those who rule!

He had special empathy with the disenfranchised
While the haughty and rich, His parables despised!
Advice to rich: "Sell what you have! Give to the Poor!"

DIFFICULT CIRCUMSTANCES

Whatever conditions are faced,
Meaning in life can be discovered!
Persistence in searching is found!

Contrasts of freedom vs. confinement,
Have key conditions that are significant!
Astounding humans are being important!

Now we do honor Nelson Mandela!
His dedication survived 27 years in prison!
He dreamed of freedom because he had vision!

Accounts of his wrongful imprisonment
Reveal the resilience of the human spirit!
Purposeful meaning can resist resentment!

There is wide variance in human justice!
Key reports reveal extraordinary endurance!
Personal integrity enhances one's resistance!

Nelson Mandela is a global example!
He became the South African President!
Contagious smile inspires our confidence!

Mandela's mission overcame apartheid!
Inspiring humanity to press to new heights!
Racial discrimination is moving toward demise!

As injustice persists, we are challenged!
Unjust persons who can do much damage!
Corrective actions demand the dedicated!

PAINFUL SUFFERING

Suffering illness and also confinement
    These conditions are miserable experiences!
      Determination to survive may be providence!

Abusive relations can become horrible!
    Many abused persons can be resourceful!
    Enduring misery that is even meaningful!

Insights about life occur in difficulties!
    Misery is an occasion to learn key lessons!
    Hard times conditioned human patience.

Numerous peoples are paid very little!
    Impoverished suffer while 1% are wealthy![5]
    Economic systems tolerate condition inequity!

Insufferable conditions exploit the vulnerable!
    Meaning uncovered can become valuable!
    Revealing deep meaning that can be enviable!

Humanity faces deplorable conditions,
    Illustrated in the starving and homeless!
    This needs to be addressed by many nations.

Failed social policies become apparent,
    So that people suffer, plus the environment!
    Humane conditions need effective governance!

Inequalities have been accumulating widely;
    Both in advanced economies with the poorly.
    Resource distribution is not done automatically.[6]

---

[5]   Putnam, op.cit.

[6]   Piketty, T. 2020 CAPITAL and IDEOLOGY, Bellnap Press of Harvard University Press.

CAUSES VS. SYMPTOMS

Charity for the poor is often encouraged,
    Assuming that the social problems are small!
      Givers feel like their contributions cover enough!

The extensive scope of the plight of the poor,
    Is much greater than only charity can procure!
    Moreover, just giving does not address causes!

Economics of the free-market is one-sided!
    It works for the wealthy but not for the plighted!
      Labor is considered a commodity that can be hired!

The term "free" infers options for choosing!
    However, "impoverished" it is more like losing!
    When costs are cut, unemployment keeps rising!

Victims of free-market economics do suffer,
    Many have no job, but expenses continue!
      Some are homeless plus being destitute!

Employed persons struggle to make ends meet!
    Those without a cushion of savings envy the elite!
    They feel like victims who also cannot compete!

Free-market favors rich and well heeled!
    Unemployed and homeless are a symptom!
    Causes are much deeper than what appears!

Charity does not address causes of poverty!
    Avoiding causes does not provide penetration!
    Even a big gift only relieves surface symptoms!

POLICY SCIENCES

In recent decades, policy sciences emerged!
    Economic, social and political issues addressed!
        A science contributes to how problems are solved!

    Globally, there are numerous fiscal phonies
    Identified in a book: _ARGUING with ZOMBIES!_[7]
    Economists identify these as new enemies!

Often legislation and remedies fight symptoms!
    These postpone solutions without penetration!
        Policy sciences demand intensive investigation![8]

    Defining problems is a key initial approach.
    Digging into causes that make the problems.
Analysis of issues becomes multi-disciplinary.

Each discovery also needs further testing!
    Is this finding a symptom or cause contributing?
        Deeper redefinitions are frequently happening!

    Initially pet or surface solutions are delayed!
    First, causal definitions; then solution considered!
Ethical and social values must also be included!

Pet solutions usually do not meet this test!
    Approaches need to be broadly comprehensive!
        Forming political coalitions can help with the rest!

    Anticipating opposition can be done helpfully!
    Testing empirically, politically and ethically,
Both short and long term goals are essential.

---

[7]   Krugman, P., 2020, _ARGUING with ZOMBIES_, W.W. Norton & Company, New York.
[8]   See Chapter 20.

Recommendations made to decision-makers,
Helpfully, convincing, brief and communicable!
Each step may require practice and rehearsal!

As objectives and goals are identified,
Evaluation processes must be provided
Strategies for introduction are identified!

CASE STUDIES

These strategies continue to be improved!
Experiences over 30 years have been tested!
Illustrating how social policy can be practiced!

Health care policy returned in the 1970's.
In the U.S. this already had a 60-year history;
I taught these approaches many semesters.

Attempts in 1910's, 30's, 60's were defeated!
In the 70's and 90's more were attempted!
Each effort provided momentum delayed!

In 2010, the Affordable Health Care Act!
Incorporating facets made it more strategic.
Still not ideal but optimal to become historic!

As Director of Contemporary Policy Studies,
Teams addressed domestic & internationally!
"Violence, Conflict & Peace" done repeatedly.

Each attempt provides important learning!
Policy is formulated over long-term researching!
Creating coalitions in democracy is necessary!

PLIGHT OF THE POOR & HOMELESS

This will illustrate complex processes.
Most social economies have homeless.
Impoverishment has long-term issues!

Using a problem-solving model,
Identifying issues and evidence,
Provides clues to its social depth!

Factors include families and resources,
Plus economics, politics and charities!
Digging deep helps to find the crises!

Needs for jobs, plus education and services:
Health care, housing, government and society!
Gaps need to be identified in problem-solving!

Research, interviews and consultations,
Plus review of existing data and solutions!
Pet solutions along with quick-fixes avoided!

Hard empirical data & ethical considerations!
Appraisal of resources that could be available!
Resistance needs to be recognized to be realistic!
Poverty and homelessness is multi-faceted!
Vested economic and politics are affected!
Tough persistence is vital in order to succeed.

Coalitions to cultivate become essential,
Including the homeless and poor is crucial!
Long-term commitment will become vital!

Even previous failures can be useful.
Assessing the political climate is essential.
After problems are defined, then solutions!

Combining compatible recommendations,
Revising, revising, revising and redefining!
Persisting patiently with this researching!

Pre-testing recommendations with panels,
Incorporating new ideas along with data.
Keeping recommendations simple and clear!

Processes can be repeated as needed,
Creative innovations being contributed!
Criticism and limitations can be recognized.

Identify social and government decision-makers,
Not forcing pre-mature needs to be anticipated!
Listening for stakeholders who are involved!

Surely, awareness of quick fixes is apparent,
Readiness to include adaptations is certain.
Keeping eyes of the goals and objectives!

This analysis is obviously now limited!
Encouragement continues to be conveyed.
Learning improvements is recommended!

You are encouraged to share ideas!
These issues need more strategies!
Build further approaches and tactics!

3. SOCIALLY

Why is hope so powerful?
    How does hope motivate us?
        Is living without hope plausible?

Hope is not a recent discovery!
    Why is hope so inspirational?
        What are your ideas while reading?

Human experience historically values hope!
    Life is better experienced by great expectations!
        Envisioning future hope requires our imagination!

"Without hope, people perish!"[9]
    "Faith, Hope and Love abide!"[10]
        Hope can actually keep us alive!

Hope inspires us to keep on trying!
    Being hopeful can keep organizations vying!
        Prolonged hopelessness becomes draining!

Poverty of hopelessness and unemployment,
    Tests humans for becoming significant!
        Otherwise we may feel unimportant!

Relationships and purpose keeps us going!
    Remember these verses to be forward looking!
        Helping us to focus when we need inspiring!

---

[9]   The Bible
[10]   First Corinthians 13

POSITIVE AND NEGATIVE
LOYAL RELATIONS

What binds people together under favorable and negative conditions?
Are there affirmations and dis-conformation dynamics or substitutions?
Once persons make commitments are there reasons to dissolve loyalty?
How do people stick together when in order to survive thick & also thin?

These relationship dynamics of loyalty are examine in various settings,
Included are martial loyalties, religious commitments & political parties.
Plus professional careers in working relationships and Doctor-patients,
Or volunteer groups along with the loyalties with buddies in the military!

Is loyalty as an ethical virtue a once and for all-time decision or choice?
When other people change their allegiance, what does one do in response?
Are human beings actually trustworthy to never leave or to forsake?
What are key cultural variables about how people consider do operate?

MARITAL TRUSTWORTHINESS

Marital trust is bolstered with cultural and personal religious values,
Ceremonies express the nature and beliefs about both husbands & wives.
Solemn vows are announced before an officiant and/or congregations,
Partners' commitment to marriage loyalties are supported by sanctions.

Family and tribal loyalties are immediately placed as center of marriage,
Each partner pledges their "Troth" to each other to leave their parents.
Solemn ceremonies typically will under-gird these critical dynamics,
"A man shall leave his Father and Mother" in order to cling to his wife!

Each partner benefits from realizing this exclusive bond to each other,
Each partner benefits from realizing that they are marrying a family also!
Legal sanctions also "shift" the life decisions about medical treatment!
While it is recommended to be inclusive, spouses hold sole commitment.

In United States, each partner is responsible to back each other's debts,
    This incurs financial responsibilities that test a couple's commitments.
Many controversies are simplified if this legal provision is explained,
    Then each partner knows that purchases are not open to be complained.

Except in cultures authorizing polygamy and polyandry as traditions,
    All other relationships are secondary so that marital are "soul relations."
"Forsaking all others" is stated explicitly in traditional ceremonies,
    These sanctions are designed to surround marriage with societal values!

Frequently couples experience stresses they may not have anticipated,
    Sorting our loyalties to each other may be helped by expert perspectives.
Marital counselors and clergy are on the front line to address conflicts,
    Partners must be transparently open and trustworthily loyal as explicit.

Extra marital sexual affairs fracture complete loyalty to each other,
    When careers compete with family life, spouse and children will suffer.
The demanding loyalty dynamics of marriage is not for everyone,
    People need to evaluate and prepare their readiness to another one!

Capt. Mark Kelly, husband of Rep. Gabby Gifford was shot in the head,
    He is a lead astronaut who is demonstrating power of marriage loyalty.
Gabby is Congresswoman surviving shots from socio-path's atrocity,
    She is nobly struggling to recover with encouragement plus dignity.

Gabby's anchor and husband, Mark, demonstrates double loyalties,
    He had been at her bedside in Arizona and Houston hospital facilities.
He is scheduled to Captain the spaceship lifting off from the Earth.
    He is not only committed to his wife, Gabby, but also to country!

The processes of healing and training are commendably noteworthy,
    They inspire each other through their highly difficult responsibility.
Their commitment to each other helped them to take very high risk,
    With each one "uplifting" the other to "lift off" then also "to live!"

POLITICAL PARTY AFFILIATIONS

An adult decision in a culture that provides elections for their leaders,
There are Independents who try to rise above any partisan loyalties,
    Is the adult identification of which political party they give allegiance.
        Are they afraid to make commitments of are they stand in judgments?

Identification with a preferred party is not always a lifetime decision,
      People grow and shift loyalties reflecting a great number of variation.
Ideologists may be loyal to a stanch of a particular party for life,
      Others may shift as they mature to address the conflicts of strife.

Standing on the fence may seem broad-minded or also standing aloof
      "Middle-of-the-Roaders" may assume themselves are decision-makers.
They are torn in directions with the winds of politics and popularity,
      Are they actually aloof and above, or are they afraid to show loyalty?

Examples of loyalty excesses are seen with two Presidents of the past,
      Lyndon Johnson thrust into office after Kennedy's assassination aghast!
He handled Legislative Branch with techniques of a political master,
      He demanded one-sided loyalty reflecting his need for political power.

Johnson was a master of foreign policy or of wartime critical decisions,
      He gathered "yes-men" who surrounded him without their criticisms.
Exuberant Hubert Humphrey was absorbed with far too much loyalty,
      Hubbie lost the Presidential election by limiting his very own credibility.

Richard Nixon was also caught in the insecurity of not trusting his staff,
      "Tricky Dick" lost his own credibility when he attempted to cover his aft!
When Watergate was uncovered, Nixon tried to deny his own complicity,
      This led to his undoing plus the fatal resignation of his own Presidency.

Lifetime loyalty in politics has many sides that lend to be analytical,
      A number of elected leaders have switched parties as they sot survival.
Self-interests are frequently dominating over values and also loyalties,
      Party switchers can both be sleazy while also facing political realities.

This dynamics identifies the need for flexibility from early loyalties,
      Political commitments are slippery when facing survival-tough realities.
Youthful decisions are important while also tentative and flexible,
      Maturity in commitments can shift in human loyalties very readily.

"Once-and-for-all-time" is unrealistic thinking blatantly and rigidly,
　　This reflects the malleability of early loyalties and political reality.
If no questions their earlier positions and their allegiance to causes,
　　This person may now be ready to be open to alternate approaches.

Beware of citizens who never evaluate their political assumptions,
　　They may be so stuck in rigidity they may also have no gumptions.
Loyalties in the political arena may best be flexible and also open,
　　Honor mature reconsiderations as they try to become transparent.

RELIGIOUS CONVICTIONS

After considering politics, is this write crazy to now look at religion?
　　Is not the personal faith decisions both private and out of tradition?
No to each previous question as we review the virtues of loyalties,
　　Religious convictions are not just private, but also valued socially.

It is surely neglectful to compartmentalize loyalties in religions,
　　Window on compartments and silos are essential for convictions.
Yes, there are personal and also social dimensions to consider,
　　To make silos of each is not being open to developments further.

Nowhere is it written that religious convictions are entirely private,
　　That is a myth protecting devotee religionists from full disclosure.
Religions have both personal and social dimensions to consider,
　　Hiding behind privacy, escapes from revealing ultimate values.

When religious people put fences or walls around their convictions,
　　Many misinterpret the breadth and scope of their religious
missions.
　　Private religion and personal spirituality sounds very appealing,
　　What do these individual loyalties demonstrate that are revealing?

Religious founders have followers who make personal commitments,
　　Buddha, Confucius, Jesus, Mohammed and other founding leaders,
Evidence of loyalties is essential for religious traditions survival,
　　All of these loyal disciples made personal decisions for revival.

Jesus had twelve Disciples whom he selected to follow him loyally,
Eleven of them continued their commitments but one was faulty.
Judas Iscariot betrayed his master at the most critical phase,
He is condemned like then as the biggest betrayer of all time.

Did other disciples desert their Master when tested under stress?
Understandably they went into seclusion full of disappointments.
Peter denied Jesus, and the others abandoned their commitments,
But loyalties to Jesus and each other bound them into missions.

Peter eventually was crucified himself in Rome with full loyalty,
Thomas allegedly took Jesus' message all the way to South India.
Phillip is accredited with traveling as a disciple into Ethiopia,
John ended his writings on the Isle of Patmos in Mediterranean.

James, Jesus' Brother, became known as Bishop of Jerusalem,
Matthew is accredited with the first Gospel account for loyalty!
There are now limited historical accounts of the other disciples,
After initial panic and bewilderment, they recruited apostles.

Why did disciples show loyalty after obvious disappointment?
Temporarily some went fishing, but soon showed commitment.
They had committed to the most important calling they knew,
With each wrenching test and trial, together a team they grew!

They apparently had loyalty to each other as the chosen few,
Except for Judas who had other ambitions, these 11 just grew!
Some had families like Peter who had a great deal to lose,
But Jesus' compelling mission, Peter could not ever refuse!

Like Paul, a loyal Apostle, Peter committed his life to Jesus,
Fishing had been his trade, but Jesus' mission was for justice!
Little he may have realized that he would become the founder
Of the Roman Catholic Church that now has become universal!

Peter was naturally emotional while Paul was just compassionate,
John was such a special disciple whom Jesus loved as mysterious!

The loyal eleven had multiple compulsions to be very dedicated,
   Their loyalty to was not only Jesus but to each other was delicate!

Like global religions, disciples' early dedication was passionate,
   Their loyalty was both to their Master but also to each other!
Since early Christian Church, there's rarely been such loyalty,
   This disciples and apostles are inspiring demonstrating fidelity!

PROFESSIONAL CAREER LOYALTY

Professional loyalty is demonstrated by many committed persons,
   They invest their energy and their creativity into the corporation.
What is remarkable is the dedication of the series of loyalties,
   Since legitimate corporations are legally defined as a person.

Employees eager for careers dedicate their energy to a mission,
   Are dramatically demonstrated by Captain Mark Kelly's position.
His powerful commitment to be a dedicated astronaut in space,
   As a Captain, his loyalty is beyond his but also in this space race.

His double commitment to Congressman Gabby and to NASA,[11]
   Shows being conditioned in the corporate culture as a passion.
This commitment is a conditional loyalty that is not eternal,
   Corporate executives may assume that every employee is theirs.

Hunan loyalties are in reality are just temporal and not eternal,
   No company merits complete employees' dedication into infernal.
Assumptions of executives may be based on a sand foundation,
   These leaders are inflated about importance for the corporation!

A critical test of loyalty occurs when there are ethical violations,
   Whistleblowers may then jump quickly into the role of salvations.
Yes, ethical convictions are paramount in employees' morality,
   There are unknown implications no individual knows entirely.

---

[11]   NASA National Air and Space Administration.

These ethical conundrums are very difficult to quickly evaluate,
   There may be vital consequences for humanity to then appreciate.
There is whistle-blowing that is based upon someone's resentment,
   When thorough investigation is done, it reveals basic commitment.

Loyalties to corporations rank lower than patriotism and family,
   Incorrect assumptions by corporate leaders have old familiarity,
Executives and managers have shallow commitments temporally,
   Companies that assume total loyalty are vulnerable personally.

Even the mission of corporation may appear to be compliable,
   These commitments are temporal and also readily so unreliable.
When companies assume they have employees' complete loyalty
   They are suffering from corporate inflation of their maternity.

While few employees may consider their company as paternally,
   When push comes to shove, their own families command loyalty.
Does any humanly created body also worth complete loyalty,
   Why do company officials consider themselves as so worthy?

Human institutions are important for even a role of temporality,
   The corporations readily assume they will be lasting for eternity!
Such inflation of importance is a human tendency to ascendancy.
   Human beings need to evaluate what does deserve their loyalty!

Who at their memorial service wish they had worked harder?
   Even patriotic & religious commitments may merit this fodder.
This may be a revelation to the misguided and over-loyalty,
   No corporate entity can promise hope for your final eternity!

DOCTOR–PATIENT

Health care professionals include nurse and various therapists,
   Their relationship with patients also is shown by psychologists.
These trusting loyalties are grounded in careful preparation,
   Professionals are licensed by states with assuring certification.

Such a trustworthy loyalty is essential for healing facilitation,
  Patients are helplessly ill needing care by healing profession.
When a patient trusts their caregiver, recovery can occur,
  If there is lack of mutual trust, healing is more uncertain.

Licensed professionals also have ethical codes for their conduct,
  Since patients are vulnerable, state controls license of a doctor.
When codes of ethics are violated, professional are to be liable,
  Law suits and disciplining are two forms of societal censure.

OBSERVATIONS

Over these examples of powerful relationship formed in society,
  The focus of this analysis has been upon the concepts of loyalty.
Loyalty: the Vesting Virtue by Ed Sultan[12] explains the dynamics,
  He also addresses that loyalties are notoriously very complicated.

Loyalties are complex because two or more relations are involved,
  For optimal outcomes, it is important to see how these evolved.
Husband and wife are obviously between two people in America,
  But the third party involved is the state to protect each legally.

So when divorce procedures start, one partner does not just quit,
  There are many implications and consequences involved in it.
Legal decisions are made about dependent children custody,
  Distributions of assets also require legal sanctions to dispose.

Other loyalties can be as complicated or often somewhat simpler,
  As employees and employers separate, there are items to consider.
Pay disposition and benefits are important decisions done better,
  Loyalties may terminate with mutual agreements done in letter.

---

[12] Sultan, E., Loyalty: the Vesting Virtue

The "Whistle-Blower" phenomena provides testy connections,
    Ethical considerations are crucial to arrive at best settlements.
Legal suits and/or publicity by media may also be involved,
    Reputations are at stake plus attempts so problems are solved.

These decisions are more complicated than many people think,
    Employers may be liable for wrong-doing to the Whistle-Blower.
On the other hand, the disgruntled employee has other options,
    Reconciliation could be explored plus wrong-doings corrections.

Doctor-Patient relations are very complex in fault-finding,
    Both parties may be compounding the disruption of healing.
Patients may not follow orders given by doctors to practice,
    Professionals may also be involved in the case as complicit.

Legal settlements are disrupting & often overrated by press,
    All parties may suffer in different outcomes to settle a case.
Mutual termination of a professional relationship can occur,
    Not all patients and all professionals might engage in a stir.

Religious and political loyalties are unique and also similar,
    Both involve values and beliefs that develop and also occur.
Loyalties are keys in commitments to each other for a time,
    Both arenas expect lifetime loyalties that change over time.

Ultimate Divine-Human relations are uniquely undertaken,
    We have assurances from God, human trust may be forsaken.
Political loyalties are obviously temporal and not eternal,
    Understandably, politics are not eternal so can be volatile.

There are numerous relationships that will not be analyzed,
    These previous illustrations can introduce to be more wise.
Human affairs do not function without a variety of loyalties,
    We are not isolated individuals but a vital part of societies!

4. FLEXIBILITY

Chameleons or chamaeleons are a distinctive and highly specialized clade of Old World lizards with 202 species described as of June 2015. These species come in a range of colors, and many species have the ability to change color. Wikipedia

GROWING ON PLAINS;
CLIMBING MOUNTAINS;
LIVING IN VALLEYS!

When I discovered my favorite rock, my imagination soared!
Having never been near mountains, I envisioned tall peaks!
My prize rock's flat bottom supported the peaks up to heaven!
Steep cliffs are carved out ledges to climb that I still admire!

These creative fantasies balanced childhood on Great Plains!
Our family farm did have those rolling hills of very fertile soils.
Our two big hills scared me while driving our team of horses!
I drove a team of two Belgium draft mares each weighing 2 tons!

I can still recall as we climbed big hills with the heavy loads,
This was "A Man's Job" both my Dad and Uncles encouraged.
I leaned over to counter shaky bumps that could tip us over!
Going downhill, I tugged the reigns for teams to go slower!

"Daise and Bell" were two mares who never birthed colts,
"Daise" had powerful muscles while "Bell" was slightly taller!
These two were my favorite pair as they did teamwork!
Neighbors would then pay me $0.25 an hour for my skills!

These farm experiences taught to do work with our team!
With my parents, siblings and uncles we all "pitched in!"

My imagination soared that climbing hills was tough work,
   As early "gifts" these times taught to never or ever "shirk!"

Attending Country School for eight years was not ever flashy!
   Elinor was my classmate who helped us working together!
I had driven her Father's team of horses for "making hay!"
   That only meant we stacked hay on wagon to take to barns.

In High School, she and I led our classmates as top students,
   No one was surprised to learn we both became educators!
Being a Farmer, a Teacher or Minister were primary models,
   Girls became farm house wives and teacher combinations.

In High School basketball was the key sport that we all played,
   My love for this game continues even now into eight decades!
I played four years with two of those as a first team forward!
   In Junior High, our team won as Champions of the County!

Teamwork was exemplified by the girls' BB winning team,
   My classmate, Arlys, played first string forward four years!
Our Girls' team won the Iowa State tournament of 600 schools,
   She scored 29 points in the Iowa Championship undefeated!

Challenged to climb an even higher peak by Texas' Governor,
   At 14, Arlys' team beat Texas team to be National Champs!
At 16, she Captained her team to become State Runners-Up!
   Six years later, we married by forming our own partnership!

By 16, she learned how to win big and to also to lose with grace!
   Forty years later, she led our partnership to even higher peaks!
In the intervening years even higher mountains were climbed!
   For life and death experiences that neither of us anticipated!

Iowa does not have mountain peaks but is tops in agriculture,
   Currently my small farm produces top rate corn yields on earth!

Intervening mountains to climb were unbelievably challenging!
Climbing gradually together from the valleys to top viewing!

These early years in the Iowa Plains are tremendously valued,
We had very typical farm and town living to be remembered!
Currently, I would not trade this learning right on the prairie!
Where people are near the soil to raise important produce!

While I continue to have this small family farm that I value,
The sentiments that were nourished there were invaluable.
We learned to "pitch-in" to get the job down however tough!
Complaints were not enough unless you were losing blood!

BEYOND THE PLAINS

My four years of conditioning was at the University of Iowa,

The state's largest university was academically challenging!

At just 17 years old competing with top students of the state,

This was stimulating as international students were present.

Conditioning to climb these academic peaks while competing,

Confidence built up by "Phi Eta Sigma" Honorary Fraternity.

Broad Liberal Arts plus a multi-disciplinary academic major,

Involved Economics, Accounting and Personnel Management.

While I was still 20, I graduated "With Highest Distinction!"

Multiple opportunities were offered to this Iowa farm lad!

Simultaneously, Arlys was my steady girl who was teaching.

Within six months, my country called me for military training!

My Air Force assignment was in Research and Development,

New Mexico was the key base for nuclear tests to be explored.

Challenging service as Squadron Adjutant with 250 men,

Promotion to Assistant Base Adjutant of over 3000 persons.

As Base "Top Secret Officer," for highly classified documents,[13]

Responsibilities involved being part of testing nuclear weapons.

These ominous challenges to sign orders for the whole base,

Was built on teamwork that scientists and crews had space.

Two mountain top experiences also happened in this tour,

Arlys and I married in Iowa onward to Albuquerque in 1955!

Moreover, the Sandia Mountains were moderate to climb.

We also enjoyed Colorado, Grand Canyon and Santa Fe.

---

[13] My Security Clearance included access to Los Alamos Atomic Research Center.

Upon release from active duty as an Officer to rejoin Bell,

This promising management position had much to tell.

In the middle of management advancement, a "Call" came,

This mysterious spiritual experience became compelling!

Rational explanations fail to capture these faith convictions,

Wrestling with positions and risks were peak experiences!

Resigning from a promisingly secure position took risks,

Entering another field of ministry led to even more peaks!

The University Administration where I enrolled then offered:

In Personnel Management as Director of Mens' Dormitories.

Opportunities unfolded Arlys and I had never envisioned,

She completed her Bachelor's Degree; I earned a Masters.

One summer, we were Manager and Counselor of a Camp,

Located in the midst of the mountains in Colorado State!

While we had numerous responsibilities to undertake,

This unique setting was natural to climb more mountains.

She hesitated to climb "Longs Peak" reaching above14,000 feet,

A young college Pre-Dent student and I undertook this feat.

The East Face was almost identical to my small favorite rock,

We mastered this climb successfully to cap another peak.

Back to the plains of Iowa, even more mountains appeared,

Our daughter was born the next year as we became parents.

This occurred during my Student Pastorate in Volga, Iowa.

Susan Louise was also baptized during that winter of 1960.

LAKES AND MOUNTAINS

Thereupon, several "calls" were extended for future ministry,
    We accepted the new call to "John Hus Presbyterian Church!"
We had captivating three years living near Lake Minnetonka,
    Minneapolis-St. Paul was Lake Country with many challenges.

This pastoral role with a Senior Minister leading was helpful,
    Orrin was grateful for assistance serving a large congregation.
The broad range of pastoral ministries was also very expansive,
    Stretching me to learn new skills with people who were receptive.

Working in partnership, we both had strengths and limitations,
    We "covered" for each other in baptisms to end-of-life funerals.
Yes, climbing was exhausting at times physically and emotionally,
    Plus parenting expanded with the arrival of our son, Gregory.

Filling roles as Chair of Presbytery Committees was demanding;
　　Mentoring and guiding candidates became a major involvement.
These committed persons were struggling with calls to ministry,
　　Most were promising while a few were obviously then not ready.

"HOLY ROLLERS"

This image may be surprising when these verses now unfold,
　　The title of "Holy Rollers" was so unusual so this now is told.
As pastor at a challenging suburban church near Minneapolis,
　　Monday mornings four of us gathered from the Metroplex.

The proprietor of a local bowling alley appreciated our work,
　　The management had free lanes so that we could "download."
Since the weekends were so loaded with demanding services,
　　With bowling balls and static pins, we released our energies!

Only informed parishioners realized the demand on a Minister;
　　These supportive lay persons helped us avoid some disasters.
With coffee and bowling, we neutralized our built up tension,
　　Even Jesus had to rest so we appreciated no apprehension.

One colleague would point to a standing single pin upright,
　　He called this a "stubborn elder" who always would fight.
By keeping composure when this battle came to a head,
　　My colleague blasted this contentious guy as he's a pin.

No, this was not a "holy" group but we did not pretend,
　　We were human in our emotions with emotions to relieve.
Supportive colleagues & lay persons make a difference,
　　So that the church's ministry handles the experience!

"EXPERIMENTAL OUTREACH MINISTRY IN BARS!"

Many persons are amazed upon learning of this experiment,
    These initial incongruities befuddled their old stereotypes.
So the context of this experience needs some clarification,
    Then these bewildered persons see this with appreciation.

While serving on the staff of a cooperative campus ministry,
    I was finishing my doctoral dissertation including a mystery.
The expanding campus at the University of Minnesota sites,
    Had the most bars, nightclubs and coffee houses in the Metroplex.

A proprietor-social worker of bars challenged our staff,
    One bar was for undergraduates serving domestic beers,
But his "Unicorn" catered to a sophisticated clientele,
    He would introduce me to a few "regulars" whom he knew.

So once a week, from about 9:00 PM until 1:00 AM,
    I visited working class bars, coffee houses and clubs.
Working alone, I would "belly up the bar" for a beer,
    He would introduce me to a bothered client he knew.

One what a Priest who came every Thursday evening,
    This was his only night off, so he felt free to do drinking.
We engaged in conversation about our mutual concerns,
    He was unburdening his cares that he carried to the bars.

He found this helpful to neutralize his responsibilities,
    Balanced and conscientious, he dealt with possibilities.
After about three beers, he could not converse further,
    So I would leave him alone and with time he sobered up.

Another was a Viet Nam Vet who just returned home,
    He fortunately was stabilized so we that could exchange.

When he left the last time, he got up about two AM,
   "Good to talk with you a human being!" his good-bye aim.

A memorable encounter was with a personnel officer,
   He was dealing with union negotiations for "3M" firm.
The bargaining was tough as he unloaded his cares,
   We both learned about how to handle our stresses.

Barmaids and Bartenders have unique insights in customers,
   They learn how to banter and also to become key listeners!
Barmaids do have mixed-up very lives so they are surprised,
   When they inquire what I was doing? With big ears and eyes.

This "Identity Moment" provides opportunities to tune in,
   When they heard I was a Psychologist listening to them.
What flipped some out temporarily I was also a Minister,
   Floods of pent-up feelings as they wanted a comforter.

Within ten years, 15,000 students would live there,
   Campus ministers learning new approaches how to share.
Barmaids were troubled with both work and their life,
   They needed attention as they just tried to survive.

Experiences helped me further learn to engage strangers,
   Unobtrusive listening is the key to hear workable factors.
Minister learn from reaching out into some strange places,
   But that is where troubled people often need their spaces.

The blessing of supportive wives and nurses are remembered,
   Without these gals at the battle scenes on the home front.
Old veterans count blessings each day to live a fuller life.
We honor the Oldest Veterans' for facing bad war strife.

I servied as a youth counselor for a Work camp in Kentucky,[14]
   Served for a week as Assistant Dean of Youth, Purdue University.

---

[14]   See Appendices for list of Retreats.

The after seven years, elected to represent Northwest Presbyteries,
  This national role involved Standard Examinations of Candidates.

During those seven years, my denomination made a challenge,
  Encouraging applications to pursue inter-disciplinary Doctorate!
Fortunately, an award for graduate study for advanced degrees,
  I pursued hard-nosed empirical study of Educational Psychology.

The University of Minnesota, known as a "hotbed of empiricism!"
  Was another Mountain in the Lake Country for these studies.

Fortunately, our family stayed in our neat Cape-Code House,
  We enjoyed the winters and summers that were expansive.

Susan and Greg thrived because of Arlys' knowledge of children,
  While mothering, she also became a support for new parents.
Her community involvements including "The YMCA" with couples,
  "The League of Women Voters" was also another key experience.

As an Interim and Campus Minister, my roles were extensive,
  My Doctorate Dissertation empirically tested student creativity.
A number of opportunities unfolded across this whole nation,
  Very challenging was extended from Austin College in Texas!

I was privileged that E. Paul Torrance[15] was my doctoral mentor,
  Serving as his Assistant for two years to learn creativity research.
This innovative Mentor guided into the new field of endeavor,
  His international reputation continues as recognized globally.

Paul's innovative conceptual thinking and empirical measure,
  Became the major resources to do my Doctoral Dissertation.[16]

---

[15] Millar G., 2007, THE CREATIVITY MAN: an Authorized Biography, Scholastic Testing Service, Inc.

[16] Middents, G., 1967, The Relationship of Creativity and Anxiety, University of Minnesota.

Fifty years later, his contributions to guiding creative talent,
  Is acknowledged by key Educators in multiple disciplines.

While Texas was not all unfamiliar to me from the time as cadet,
  Arlys prepared our children to anticipate a Greater Southwest!
We surprisingly built a new ranch style house for family living,
  Another couple bought our Minnetonka house briefly bidding.

Thereupon we ventured to Texas that provided opportunities,
  Austin College combined both Psychology and also Ministries.
On the Faculty of the Psychology Department, plus more roles,
  I became the Director of two credible Counseling Centers!

Our home in Sherman was impressive from its original design,
  The children loved being reared with horses for them to reign.
Arlys discovered a Pre-School for which she became Director,
  She introduced the community to League of Women Voters!

Experiences at conferences in New Orleans and Las Vegas,
  Plus mentoring graduate and also undergraduate students!
Our family also became acquainted with Margaret Crow,
  Unbelievably, Margaret became the angel for our future.

A month in Europe in 1972 was also another mountain peak!
  Plus two January Swiss seminars to learn Jung's Psychology.
The Alps not only are "The Top of the World" in Europe,
  These mountains also are the creative grounds for research.

Piaget[17] in the University of Geneva in "Genetic Epistemology,"
  Provided complementary cognitive stages developmentally.
Combining Creativity and Epistemology philosophically,
  My dual fields of Theology and Psychology now are related!

---

[17]   Piaget, J., <u>The Psychology of Genetic Epistemology.</u>

IMBIBING WITH GUYS AND GALS

Throughout eras, there are different modalities for equilibrium,
  Each approach possesses unique pluses and had also minuses.
In order to regain balance, it is essential to exercise strong legs,
  But physical strength is insufficient so others have advantages.

In past decade, our coffee clutch at the YMCA is delightful,
  Y's men and Y gals engage with repartee that is very helpful.
After ten years, we surmise many touchy topics that irritate,
  So we avoid these delicate issues unless we want to use bait.

Rarely in a group of four to ten are personal issues discussed,
The bantering is often on immediate impressions re-digested.
Since delving below polite surfaces is not pursued at the "Y."
  The bearing of one's soul is unlikely to be done by gal or guy.

Birthday events are primetimes to be engaged with friends,
  With young and seniors, we can tell our stories without ends.
Here is goes Tom, on your 87th birth when you were born,
  Let us reminisce about our trials highlighting our on the farm.

Tom has participated in at least four of the imbibing groups,
  He comes with a smile, beautiful flowers, and often good food.
We love to converse about the whole world's challenges,
  Addressing the "Big Picture Issues" rather than small ones.

MILITARY VETERANS

Own venue is with Happy Warriors composed of military Vets,
  We meet once a month for lunch, stories, programs but no bets.
The best stories are told by the combat veterans of WW II,
  They have heroic experiences that are embellished-through.

These men in their tenth decade retell their personal accounts,
  Finding a friendly audience of listeners who also have stories.
At lunch, sad stories are not typically related to save appetites,
  But in the ensuing program hours, we learn of major raw hurts.

This group of 150-175 has family members help to walk as escorts,
  There are noticeable expressions of happy release from the scars.
Some have not told their intimate friends about what was worse,
  Here is congenial atmosphere of comrades no need to rehearse.

Gatherings remind "Happy Warriors" of their Officers' Club.
  The Navy has clubs like the Army, Air Force and also Marines.
After an official debriefing, then real de-briefings emerge,
  Even crucial decisions are walked through to the very edge.

Most are grateful they returned from horrendous battles alive,
  Buddies are remembered from recollections who did not survive.
The memories of these comrades stick with vets for a lifetime,
  These sacrifices in prime years demand gratitude in our time.

Many older vets recall having to dampen raw nerves with drinks,
  The debriefings after combat included time, but not by "shrinks."
Now we hear of Post-Traumatic Stress Syndromes to fear,
  But "shell shock" and "foxholes" civilians never had to bear.

As comrades get together for drink, food and entertainment,
  Teamwork is facilitated that is natural for the next assignment.
Those who did not come back are remembered with honor,
  Because sacrifice for America is worthy for all to consider.

PROFESSORIAL TYPES

Few of my professor comrades are the Veterans who served,
These seasoned "Old Profs" appreciate our history in reverse.
We look back from now to where we have served and taught,
Remembering old military stories both laden and also fraught.

After decades of teaching students with our recollections,
We predominantly are gratified with their contributions.
The mounting rewards know realizing "Teaching is Eternal!"
We have invested ourselves in the past and into the future.

Now stories by "Old Profs" are parallel to those of veterans,
We survived decades of challenges of these new generations.
We may start to sound like an "Echo Chamber" with stories,
But the accumulated gratification is hardly ever equaled.

The metaphor of battles is tempered with struggles of minds.
Internal wounds of cogitations leave involve enlarging brains.
We are thankful for God-given gifts that are multiplying now,
So our fellowship combined recollections with those endowed.

Stimulation with knowledgeable colleagues is very satisfying,
We learn from each other with encouraging and confronting.
Few professions provide long-term fulfillment and gratitude,
Our combined perspectives multiply these types of attitude.

Gourmet Dinner Groups
Twelve couples now belong to one gourmet social group,
One has been continuously meeting monthly for 30 years.
We rotate in dining by meeting at homes for fellowship,
Each couple prepares special ingredients for table talk.

Now a smaller group of five couples prescribe new recipes,
  We live in three different counties so we meet quarterly.
The intimacy of the smaller group has obvious advantages,
    All conversations are shared openly rather than selectively.

Food and wine provide the key ingredients to this sharing,
  We all have grandchildren, so no baby-sitters are waiting.
When there are illnesses or losses we all suffer together,
  Such supportive friends make an immense get-together.

Learning about the special foods of different cultures,
  We expand our appreciation for traveling adventures.
Each time we have new experiences with acquaintances.
  We have not traveled together in these new ventures.

We hear about the adventures that colleagues are taking,
  With spouses along, the excitement finds real balancing.
We all learn vicariously as others describe experiences,
  This provides secondary pictures of many other cultures.

II. GLOBALLY

5. INTERNATIONALLY

Rotary International

As a Rotarian for over 44 years that is benefits mutually,
   Key leaders in a community find a variety occupationally.
"Service Above Self" [18]provides our motto for guidance,
   Rotary International is among the finest to advance.

Projects undertaken are bold and surprising to learn about,
   Participating in these projects automatically shows clout.
Joint global partnerships provide benefit to all concerned,
   With over 1,300,000 members in 32,000 clubs that discern.

The "Four-Way Test"[19] gives broad guidelines for decisions,
   While not perfectly re-stated, all clubs provide education.
The four principles provide clear questions to consider,
   By raising penetrating principles around the whole world.

From educational projects that address human problems,
   The combined strengths of groups to not live in a vacuum,
Having been awarded two University Teachers Grants,
   I appreciate the Rotary impact, plus some contrarians.

Polio Plus inoculations have been undertaken for 30+ years,
   Other vaccines make the "Plus" that will prevent diseases.
More than a half billion dollars have been raised to spend,
   Building not only health but world-wide in places abroad.

---

[18]   Sheldon, A.F., 1911, "Rotary's two Official Mottoes," Awarded to the Author in 2000.
[19]   Principles of Rotary International.

India with over 1.2 billion people, 250,000,000 inoculated,
  Three years later, over 125,000,000 preventions provided.
Presently, two nations have polio: Pakistan and Afghanistan;
  With further efforts, they could be free from polio again!

In 2004, we had a Medical Mission to India and Viet Nam,
  Jointly inoculating 30 million more plus supplies for humans.
These preventive measures are most useful strategies,
  More global efforts are part of the mission of Rotary.

YOGI'S YOGA

For nearly 20 years, I have enjoyed Yoga lead by David,
  Our sessions are twice a week which balances exercises.
We warm-up with stretches and breathing very deeply,
  We do not pretend to be experts nor men who are holy.

Colleague Tom with whom we traveled to India in 2004,
  That the holier a Holy Man is, the less clothes cover!
Tom, Carol and I with Rotarians to inoculate children,
  For the "Last Push in Polio Plus" covering thirty million.

Our previous travels to India and Nepal in 1995, 1998, 2001;
  Carol and I learned Urdu words with this pleasant surprise.
In Yoga we greet each other with "Namastae" each time,
  This is a cordial greeting and salutation people feeling fine.

When I was invited to fill "The UNESCO PEACE CHAIR;"
  I relearned that in Hindu, the term Shanti means Peace.
An invitation also came from the CSI[20] Bishop of Mangalore,
  Preached at his diocese Church named "Sushanti"-Good Peace!

---

[20] Church of South India where I was invited to teach in Kerala and Manipal
  University in Karnataka.

At YMCA yoga class, David leads us in repeating "<u>Shanti</u>,"
By the end of an hour's class, we relax to also meditate.

Then a small group of participants from a class of 15-20,
We did enjoy imbibing coffee to top off our exercise day!

Yoga serves as a balance for me with its silent stretches,
Meditation and breathing are only two of the benefits.
Breathing air deeply plus keeping my core in better shape,
Yoga's side-benefits attract people who want to relate.

ISLAMIC MEDIEVAL AND POST-MEDIEVAL SOCIETY

Most people may have puzzlement about this group's label,
Let me explain these colleagues who are dedicated Muslims.
My acquaintance with these professionals in 1998 began,
When I first met Ambassador Syed Ahsani of Pakistan.

He and I had discussions at Central Mosque of Dallas,
My curiosity was about Pakistan before going to India.
He had been an Ambassador to Afghanistan and Brazil,
Since then we have had friendly exchanges ever since.

Edward Thomas was a colleague, U.S. State Department,
The Ambassador headed another regional association.
He headed the Islamic Association for the Southwest,
Consequently, I invited both to address our Dialogues.

In exchange, I was invited to join another local chapter,
The Islamic Medieval and Post-Medieval Society in D-FW.
This group has concerns to educate Americans further,
About the contributions of Islam's Golden Age period.[21]

---

[21]   Ahsani, Syed and Basheer Ahmed, 2008, <u>The Golden Age of Islam.</u>

We met monthly in exploring more educational programs,
   Members included authors, professors and global scholars.
Conference were attended for mutual support of educators,
   Efforts were made to inform the public and also teachers.

Efforts were made to sponsor a major traveling museum,
   This originated in Timbuktu, Algeria in the Sahara Desert.
Short courses are also offered to Teachers who educate,
   Plus engaging youth in essay contests about the Golden Age.

"FDIC"

First, this abbreviation represents another group designation,
   The FDIC is not for Federal Deposit Insurance Corporation.
FDIC stands for 'Food, Drink and Intelligent Conversations;'
   This is the most recent collection of imbibers established.

Men in Collin County invited me to moderate their meetings,
   After a colleague from UT Dallas[22] did this recommending.
These guys love to talk about puzzling issues of wide range,
   Apparently they met in business affairs that are not strange.

These are working professionals who are mature and curious,
   After having an evening drink and meal that is very delicious.
We spend two hours exploring topics of interest to them,
   Included are psycho-social issues, economics and religion.

"The End of the World" was an initial concern for May 21st
   When the world did not expire, now October 21 is forecast.
During intervening months, issues have varied very diversity,
   "Dispensationalism" to "Biblical Interpretation" seen widely.

---

[22]   University of Texas, Dallas where I was invited as a Guest Lecturer.

These men have wide experiences appreciating differences,
    Some are regular church-goers while others are indifferent.
I was pleasantly discovering that this is a men's support group,
    From different corporations plus community organizations.

Several sell health and life insurance with very skillfully,
    This group provides an outlet for them to process more fully.
Men cannot talk about personal worries with organizationally,
    But outside their Corporation they can share confidentially.

COMMONALITIES

Obviously, by imbibing with guys and gals has commonalities,
    An obvious one is the span of age that has clear similarities.
Occasionally a younger generation engages our visitations,
    These new faces are enjoyed providing neat variations.

Another feature is that we have complementary experiences,
    Some are in engineering, some in health fields most retired.
This expands our appreciation as we all support education,
    So these interactions provide times to mix expectation.

These is also a limited range of values and religious faith,
    Most are in Christian traditions with latitude and space.
Rigid beliefs are not present and few dietary restrictions,
    But this places limited parameters for cultural expansions.

Almost all are American citizens within one racial background,
    So these gourmet groups have limits in enlarging our bonds.
The Bar Ministry and Vet's "Happy Warriors" have variations,
    But we are all true American citizens with similar allegiances.

Educators usually have readiness to expand their horizons,
    Others display similar curiosity from various professions.

Spouses are typically both interested in fostering fun,
   Singles and widowed are naturally included for a whirl.

Gathering with familiar friends is indeed a neat blessing,
   Learning about the new developments is always informing.
These intimate interactions are prized now as so precious,
   Memories are enlarged and the meals are very delicious!

On birthdays we remember our past with real gratitude,
   For memorable experiences that come from our attitude.
As a balance, envisioning our future as life is unfolding,
   We process our past, present and future by envisioning.

Let us continue as comrades while we run in our course,
   We have both been involved in commendable professions,
With continuing commitment to honor God and humanity,
   Our fulfillment is shared both locally and also globally.

6. INEQUALITIES

We are not alone when we have faith, family and friends,
   They are likewise very saddened by our loss occurrences.
Unbelievable understanding helps to then face living alone,
   Until these are personally experienced, just then imagine.

The future was so unclear than ever before in my living,
   Yes, I had experienced mild depressive episodes before.
But the loneliness that occurred was not even anticipated,
   So "starting a new life" is both awesome plus exciting!

"The Lord Giveth and the Lord Takest Away" for always.
   These life lessons are new for each person in our days.
While these are not pleasant experiences to anticipate,
   These are the reality of living and dying on this earth!

But these are also exciting and uplifting to those peaks,
  Like flying over the mountainous terrain in an airplane,
We soar above the highest peak unaware of climbing,
  This airplane typically sores at 35,000 feet altitude.

There are not peaks on this planet that reach that,
  Even Mt. Everest in Nepal is above over 29,000 feet.
Modern airlines permit us to soar above mountains,
  Plus clouds and thunderheads into atmospheric areas.

Such experiences have happened in the last 80 years,
  Lifting planes above bad weather and also peaks!
Then astronauts have explored space to the moon,
  Now astronomers probe galaxies far, far beyond!

But gravity of this earth is tough to lift us upward,
  Gravity always works to keep us down onto earth!
Without gravity we could not survive on this planet,
  Important but not the final word into outer space!

What is "Finality" in this existence we have on earth?
  While gravity helps us survive here; What is beyond?
Myths and religious faiths addressed the speculations,
  Probing beyond this existence by imagining heavens!

Do the mythical existences have their mountain peaks?
  Are there valleys of flowers with all living creatures?
These questions are beyond scientific empirical tests,
  Dimensions of faith provide imagined these habitats!

Human imaginations are vast not about all creation!
  Our human metaphorical images are approximations!
Faith provides these assurances beyond empirical tests,
  This is beyond our desire for concrete empirical facts!

Where is the proverbial Gate of St. Peter into space?
    Where are the foisted hell fires so vividly portrayed?
While human imaginations are fascinating to behold,
    Concrete scientific evidence is now beyond this world.

The "Dark Valley" is a metaphor appealing to images.
    "The Shadow of Death" suggests beyond ethereal space.
No one with credible evidence has been to hell and back;
    While exaggerated claims have influenced the helpless.

Are there peaks and valleys in existences lying beyond?
    Do earthly human imaginations have special models?
Empirically scientific data is not available to consider,
    This leaves the contrived imaginations to then deliver!

Who can contemplate the challenges out there beyond?
    Experiences and education are helpful but not enough!
Until we personally are faced with the reality of death,
    We may best only have some secondhand knowledge!

JONAH, JOB AND JERRY

Biblical Analogy

Many people know the story of Jonah!
            He ran from God's call!
            He escaped on a ship that soon faced a storm!

In desperation, the crew asked Jonah to pray to his God!
            But the vicious Sea prevailed to their dismay!
The sailors cast traditional lots to decide guilt!
            Guilty loser: JONAH!

Jonah who was asleep!
Was he in another world?
So they cast him overboard!
Good riddance for this escapee!

This story is seen by J.W. Whedbee as comedy![23]
Reluctant Jonah tries to flee!
But a Great Whale swallowed him whole with glee!!
What a horrid place to be!

Three days and nights!
In the belly of The Whale!
Captain Ahab in Melville's <u>Moby Dick</u>![24]
In the modern opera, you feel aboard scanning the horizon!
(The staging is magnanimous!)

Everyone survives in this operatic rendition!
This plot is typical of a comedy production!
(Whoever wrote Jonah made a creative construction!)

Now permit comical humor:
This is a BIG FISH!
No scales! No photo! But a huge sketch!
This enormous fish sketch weighed eight pounds!
Even God speaks to this fish!

e.e.cummings also composed an hilarious drama"
"It Should Happened to a Dog!" is Jonah plight!
This modernized version is a playful delight!

e.e.cummings portrays Jonah as a traveling salesman!
His assigned territory of Nineveh is a tough assignment!

---

23   Whedbee, J.W., 2002, <u>The Bible and the Comic Vision,</u> Minneapolis: Fortress Press.
24   Melville, H., <u>Moby Dick.</u>

Jonah encounters many difficulties:
"What happens to Jonah shouldn't happen to a dog!
Praying to the Lord:
I called to the Lord in my distress,
And He answered me!

Out of the belly of Sheol, I cried for help!
And Thou hast heard my cry!
Thou didst cast me into the depths, far out at sea!
And the flood closed round me!

But Thou didst bring me up alive from the pit, O Lord.
As my senses failed me, I remembered the Lord
And my prayer reached Thee in Thy Holy Temple!

Men who worship false gods may abandon their loyalty!
But I offer Thee sacrifice with words of praise!
I will pay my vows; victory to the LORD! Jonah 2: 1-9."

This imaginary whale gets sick of Jonah!
So he is vomited up on the Mediterranean Shore!
Imagine the slime from this gut heaved on the beach!

From his routine life, Jonah is prodded onward!
Reluctantly, he journeys for day 'til he sees Nineveh!
Three days journey just to cross this vast city!

Jonah prophetically proclaimed:
"In 40 days Nineveh shall be overthrown!"
To Jonah's surprise, the Ninevites believed!
The King striped off his clothes, he had sackcloth!

Ninevites also put on sackcloth!
They fasted! No people or beast to eat or drink!
At the brink, they abandoned their wicked ways!

But Jonah was greatly displeased and angry!
He had escaped from his hometown, Tarshish!
Realizing the Lord is compassionate and long-suffering!

Jonah wants the Lord to take his life!
"I should be better dead than alive!"
Irony and parody, Jonah is bewildered with success!

Frustrated Jonah, makes a shelter!
The Lord makes a gourd tree to shade him!
Jonah is thankful; but the next morning;
The Lord let the gourd tree go withering!

In this heat, Jonah has another death wish!
"Why are your angry?" The Lord asks.
"Yes, I am mortally angry!" states disturbed Jonah
"I shaded you! Should you not be sorry?

"For the 120,000 of Nineveh who do not know their right hand
from their left, plus cattle without number!"

"Are you more concerned about the gourd tree?
Than repentant, fasting people in sackcloth?
Where is your empathy for my creatures?

REFLECTIONS

This story in the Old Testament is mysterious!
Is this tragedy? Parody? Provocative Prophesy?
Can the account of Jonah be humorous comedy?

People are captivated by e.e.cummings' drama!
"It Should Happen to a Dog!"
Young people love to enact and discuss it!

Simple props: Jonah looks desperate!
   The Lord expects obedience and gets rebellion!
      Imaginary boat, storm, cast over board!
   Gulped up by a Humongous Whale!
People who recall "JAWS" and shiver with fright!

Think of the themes:
   A call from the Lord; reluctance; fleeing;
      Crisis at sea; cast out; repentance! Obedience!

Jonah faced experienced stress!
   Expected to leave his home in Amattai!
      His assignment was to the foreign Nineveh!
   Escaping to Joppa to board a sea boat!
Cast overboard, swallowed by a whale!

Being sent on to heathen!
      Are they more evil than Sodom and Gomorrah?
         Tough territory for a traveling salesman!

Big city for a guy from a little community!
   Will I get into trouble? Be arrested? Beaten?
      Lord, death would be better!

Do you see Jonah as self-centered? Egocentric?
Certainly he could not be narcissistic?
But consider the irony of this reluctant prophet:
   He is successful but hates his achievement!

"OK, Lord! You saved little ole' me,
But how can you forgive Ninevites?"
   Deliverance is for my people, not foreigners!
   My hometown will ridicule my efforts!

Compassionate Lord confuses Jonah!
  We are the Chosen! They are the outside heathen!
    Are you concerned with them? Who else?
    "Lord, you have to be fair, consistent & dependable!"

What will be Jonah's future?
  Provocative literature prompts us to think?
    What do you think now?

THE DRAMA OF JOB

Consider now the suffering of Job!
  He was wealthy, comfortable and "blameless!"
    Plus a large family composed of animals and slaves!
      An unusual drama unfolds in the "Heavenly Court!"

  While reviewing the earth,
  The Lord is pleased with his servant, Job!
He asked Satan to consider Job, His prize creation!

Satan quickly responds with this challenge:
  "Do you think Job is not God-fearing for nothing?"
  "Have you not "hedged" Job with lush protection?"

The Lord agreed to do testing of Job's loyalty:
  Sabeans and Chaldeans struck like a whirlwind!
    Swept away to the four corners of the earth!
      Job loses his family, possessions and his health!

Satan pushed the Lord further:
  "Skin for skin; Job will fold if his body is stricken!"
    Hesitantly, the Lord permitted body sores to reek!
      "But spare Job's life!"

Even Job's wife advised: "Curse God and die!"
But Dear Old Job's integrity was not shaken!
Even when his suffering became intensely stressful!

Rejected and abandoned with torture,
His three long-time friends traveled to visit him!
For seven days & nights that sat silently with Job!

Thereafter, Eliphaz, Bildad and Zophar gave free counsel:
Moralizing! Moralizing! Moralizing!
Job defends himself while regretting he was born!
These three self-appointed Judges render verdicts:
"Guilty, Not Guilty! Retrial!'

After retorting with friends,
His friends pronounce their verdict: GUILTY!
Suffering is to be Job's sentence!

In a senior course in Homiletics:
My wise Professor assigned a topic with which to wrestle!
"When Suffering Cannot Be Explained!"
Pressure! Pressure! Pressure!

Job was my primary Old Testament source!
This assignment was valuable as a pastor!
Parishioners want help when they suffer!
How can we humanly withstand suffering?

Full course load; plus two part-time jobs!
A congregation plus supervising 200 dormitory residents!
New Father; Interviewing for positions; "Candidating!"
Is there light at the end of the tunnel?

But Job appeals to the Heavenly Court!
Job argues with the Lord who cross-examines Job!
This becomes a huge Courtroom trial!
Job provides consolation!

Job asks: "Why? What's next? How much stress?"
Family, Faith, Mentor and Friends help!
Divine Insights! Testing is finished!
"Magna Cum Laude" with Masters of Divinity!

For Job, Elihu appears!
Previously three old Sages! Now who?
Elihu is a young upstart giving unsolicited advice!

Three old friends plus Elihu!
All are full of old answers for Job!
But they are not open to new questions!

In our contemporary insights,
Wisdom came from Earl Weaver
Who is a notorious Baseball Coach!

Here is insight from this Sage in sports:
His book: _What I Learned After I Knew It All!_
Humble Wisdom to address new challenges!

Self-righteousness is a pitfall!
Human beings do not know it all!
Our challenges involve new dilemmas!

God interrogates Job again:
"Where were you when I laid the earth's Foundations?
"Do you have arms like God?"
"Can you thunder with a voice like His?

Divine questions respond to human accusations!
Did the Creator God bring chaos, not order?
Did He bring darkness, not light?

Death, not Life?

Irony poses juxtapositions as polarities!
God is both profound and also playful!
Is God wicked and you, Job, innocent?

Job is silent!
But silence is not enough!
Repentance is essential for reconciling!

Job's confessions:
"I talked about what I did not know!"
"I had heard about You by hearsay!
Now my eyes see You face-to-face!!"

FROM TRAGEDIES TO RESISTANCE TO RESTORATION

In comedy and parody, a "U" depicts movement:
Starting with "Prosperity;"
Then the depths of "Tragedy!"
Finally restored to a "Happy Ending!"

First movement is normal living,
Then exhausted by stressful experiences,
Recovery may have several variations.

A stressed person may be traumatized!
They may return to normal functioning!
Or positive growth may be experienced!

When Surgeons consider their sick patient:
They hope the person will be resilient!
Research reveals three general patterns,
Studies in carefully controlled research.

Two independent variables are studied:
How my pain medication is requested in recovery,
How long before a patient is discharged!

The "tough patient" assumes quick recovery:
They hardly hear what to expect in recovering!
They are difficult and demanding of nurses!

By learning from old expectations.
They used more pain medications,
And there hospital stay is longer!

The "overwhelmed patient" worries endlessly:
They are scared, distressed and vulnerable.
They want more medication and stay longer.,

The "moderately worried," listen carefully,
They request even less pain medication!
Generally, they are discharged earlier!

Modern inequalities occur world-wide;
Plus right in America where we reside.
These are now depicted by researchers;[25]
Revealing current centuries are disturbers.

In 1870-80's, huge monopolies developed;
Railroad Mongols controlled big wealth!
They possessed railroad transportation;
While they supervised large companies.

---

[25]   Putnam, op.cit. 2020

Then legal provisions for corporations;
Owners of stock provided limited liability.
Stockholders avoided key responsibility;
While users risked staying healthy.

Accidents could not be the basis for suits;
Bad corporate decisions avoided these.
Huge wealth was accumulated by a few;
Economic inequalities but no one did sue.

But in the early 1900's, new trends developed
Americans become economically more equal.
Putnam[26] traces this pattern very clearly;
He shows these patterns graphically.

In WW I, many military deaths occurred
Both Americans and Europeans suffered.
But equalities persisted economically;
Providing a better sense of real equality.

The Economic Depression of the 1930's
It occurred when I was just a baby.
On our farm, we had good supplies;
But that did not occur for many families.

Then World War II required heavy debt;
Europeans and Americans had many regrets.
While defeating the Germans and Japanese
All nations involved had very heavy losses!

Recoveries were slow in much of the world;
Americans had to learn how to manage.
Economic equalities persisted into 1960's.
Thereafter, United States has inequalities.

---

[26] Op.cit., 2020, Putnam, R., The Upswing, Simon and Schuster, New York.

7. RACIALLY

Cultures vary about how lies and truths are handled!
  Moral standards may be different for our native land!

There shame cultures in which sanctions disapprove!
  These sanctioning controls may not be internalized!

Another type of culture is known as a guilt society!
  Persons internalize acceptable standards for guides!

Children who are in a guilt culture gradually learn!
  Those in a shame culture may lie unless criticized!

Western cultures typically tend to be guilt societies,
  Other cultures process truth and falsehood differently!

Problems occur as cultures interact to be clashing!
  So that contracts and statements may be puzzling!

Judicial processes vary in different justice systems,
  Being aware of these difference help with practices!

AMERICAN PATTERNS OF TRUTHFULNESS

The basic guilt culture of America varies widely,
  Immigrants enter bringing their values socially!

Native Americans, Christians, Jews and Muslims,
  Generally internalize this morality as children!

Inconsistencies occur that disturb interactions!
  Justice processes attempt to take jurisdiction!

In most families and school, standards are learned,
  By early school years, guilt has been internalized!

Corrections reinforce behavior if done consistently,
  So expect variations among people interactively!

Of course, practices are not always dependable,
  Legal and police officials make laws enforceable!

AMERICAN JUDICIAL PROCESSES

Many persons believe that children do not lie!
  This is an uninformed position that they comply!

Research demonstrates naïve' persons may lie,
  If trusted persons share untruths as believable!

Susceptible adults can be gullible to a "story!"
  Both believing an untruth but embellishing it!

Parents have had their children taken into custody,
  If inexperienced prosecutors exercise authority!

When their children fess up that they had lied,
  Family custody is then supposed to be restored!

Gossip is a vehicle to transmit feasible tales!
  As transfers occur, receivers hear differently!

Many investigators use polygraphs as tests,
  But such evidence if not permitted in trials!

Polygraphs do not meet legal standards of truth,
  As physiological measures can be inconsistent!

Police find the polygraph useful in another way,
   Some suspects confess believing detectors work!

Employers may use polygraph for job screening,
   Giving impressions the results will be revealing.

Swearing in a witness to tell the whole truth
   is not assurance sociopaths will be compliant!

Consequently, corroborating testimony is essential,
   Counter a liar's story particularly for its potential.

Pathological lying is difficult to otherwise detect!
   Stressed out witnesses may not have accurate truth!

HOW AND WHY DO PEOPLE LIE?

A writer from India suggests way to detect lying!
   The 12 indicators are also hypotheses for testing!

1. *Watch a person's eye contact may detect dishonesty!*
   Staring or shifty often over-compensating full eye contact!

2. *If a person gulps audibly may also disclose trouble!*
   They may lubricate or clear their throat as tensions builds!

3. *When a liars shakes his head opposite to what they say!*
   Momentarily hesitating to nod or shake their head sway!

4. *Touching their nose often is a clue to give them away! Watch*
   physical movements as shifting can reflect a lie!

5. *Unconsciously touching/covering a mouth is a clue! Pursing their*
   eyes may unconsciously to conceal a lie!

6. Split-second change in expression may give them away! Eyebrows furrowed upward making lines in their forehead!

7. Breathing faster while lying can reveal fabrications! Unless they have just been in a fast marathon running.

8. Frequently repeating a phrase or facts can revel lying! Trying to over-emphasize points may not be convincing!

9. If their voice is faster or slower, higher or lower! Talking at a very fast pace or talking even faster!

10. Outlandish details are common when exaggerating! Details that are "over the top" can reveal compensating!

11. Watch their hands as they may disclose untruthfulness! Scratching, touching one's nose or lips or clenching fists!

12. Leaning in if frequently associated with honesty, Leaning back or away is a posture of lying frequently!

    Testing out these twelve indicators in collecting details, Helps inexperienced persons to be suspicious in many ways!

    No one exclusive way can uncover persistent fabrication! But better detections may occur with multiple observations!

HOW ARE YOU DOING?

How are you doing?
Are you down and sad?
Are your happy or glad?
These are questions?
Depend on perception!

Fortunately people ask
  Quick, easy and also fast!
    Usually these are friendly,
  Almost asked superficially!
Asking how you feel really?

There are wide responses!
  Depends on circumstances!
    Should I be quick or shallow?
  How do I know this fellow?
Now wanting to be callow!

If a friend then one thing.
  If a stranger another thing!
    If a Doctor, something deeper!
  If Minister, more to consider!
If family, even more sincere!

SUPERFICIAL OR SINCERE?

Are you happy or sad?
  Are you wary or mad?
    When can you say "Glad?"
  Or share personal insights,
May there be some slights?

Often questions are greeting!
  These conservations are fleeting!
    Few really want to know feeling!
  This depends who are meeting!
Is there time to do explaining?

Assessing these circumstances,
  Is essential for your answers!

Is this just a quick hit and run?
Does the occasion call for fun?
Depends on what is the forum!

Can they handle sad depression?
Or close up with quick succession?
Who really understands feelings?
Confidences about these dealings?
Will they continue with meetings?

Of course, many want to happy!
They hesitate to feeling sadly!
Happy is personally subjective.
Not expecting to be objective;
Prompting both to be reflective.

HAPPINESS

Many persons want to be happy!
However, life deals with reality!
Happy was for Greek Philosophy,
As well as dispositions in History!
While actual living is sad and happy!

What is a definition of happiness?
Satisfaction? Feelings? Readiness?
Understandably people are hesitant
To share what might be discontent!
Is it right now, or full development?

Contrasted with feeling sadness,
Is one definition of happiness!
Is there depth to this readiness?
Most people value friendliness
Reserving truth with willingness!

Experiences vs. immediate responses
Is key contrast with their performance.
People search for their own importance!
Hoping that they will have satisfaction
Rather than feeling sheer exhaustion!

MEANINGFUL PURPOSES

Deeper ideas involve purposefulness!
Plus an inner self of meaningfulness!
People do not want to feel usefulness!
Prompting avoidance of hopelessness
Deeply desiring a sense of worthiness!

Engaging in challenges is essential
So that others see it is beneficial!
Investing our energy is then crucial
To be uplifting, important to others
As we consider our sisters & brothers!

As we review our lives in retrospect
We hope to be treated with respect!
Helping the helpless is respectable
As we assist them in becoming able!
It is timely in trying to be available.

Doing both treatment and prevention
Is important for us to give attention!
Band-Aids can help in emergencies
But long-run solutions cure crises!
Our efforts how we invest ourselves!

SO HOW ARE WE DOING?

A key ingredient is mutuality!
If we have hope to live joyfully!
We do need to feel hopefully!
Resulting in both having respect!
This is what human beings expect.

A special challenge is the loner
Who is hesitant to be a talker!
Listening with a keen third ear
Might help but not interfere!
Loners want to feel you hear.

This requires efforts in patience
Because trust has to be established!
When persons have a feeling of safety
Mutual sharing is much more likely!
So it is best not to be in a hurry!

Patient give and take in exchanges
So that mutuality has better chances!
Both can then experience significance
That is so important to find meaning.
Each feels like a person not just a thing!

LET'S GIVE THIS A TRY

Human have importance inherently!
Life is not fatal; It happens miraculously!
A human being is extremely complicated!
Life needs to be relationally recognized!
One's very existence is to be prized!

Persons can live in blighted conditions
Hopefully they survive in these options.
Many discover meaning while suffering
Particularly if they have socializing.
People help people can be surprising!

It is helpful if people discover hope!
This ingredient helps them to cope!
So do not give up but be involved!
People help problems to be solved!
Naturally it's essential to be resolved!

Let us join together in helping out!
Even when we may have some doubt!
Optimism is better than pessimism
Thereby may we discover wisdom.
Let us have a favorable disposition!

HOW IS "IST" DEFINED?

"Possibilitist" describes Hans Rosling[27] recently,
He is seen as a "Poet of Percentages" statistically!
Hans refines his image as not being an optimist,
He takes emotions apart as a statistical analyst!

"IST" does not infer primary principal or first!
Neither is the opposite of IST called the worst!
Rather than first, IST is usually the last syllable,
Frequently this term enhances as an "enablist!"

Initially, to orient you readers, I am a generalist!
These perspectives derive out of broad interests.

---

27   Cristakis, Nicholaus A., April 30, 2012, "Hans Rosling: Poet of Percentages as Statistician," <u>Newsweek.</u>

Contrary, wide experiences as an experimentalist!
  Vast angles are visualized, but not as a specialist!

I quickly perceive "a little about a lot" as I resist
  Concentrating on one specialized field to persist.
Considering myself a "bridge-builder for peace,"
  Discovering we will have peace without justice.

Nor am I considered the dumbest or smartest,
  Building bridges places me right in the midst.
Trying to connect extreme as leftist or rightist,
These polar opposites fail to resolve but resist.

IN THE MIDST OF POLAR OPPOSITES!

"ISTs" in the world exert influence us as realist,
  Prompting me to redefine how I presently exist!
These verses may help to prompt self-definitions,
  Patient is needed than becoming an abolitionist!

I describe myself as a professional Psychologist!
  But I am not a specialist, but rather a Therapist!
Neither do I considered myself as a pessimists,
  Instead my self-perception is to be an optimist!

Neither am I considered to be a negative fatalist,
  But rather my faith guides me to be a Biblicist!
God's Sovereignty includes pre-destinationalist,
  My human limits are an uncertain universalist!

The term fundamentalist does not apply to me,
  Neither do I feel like an opportunistic terrorist!
Nihilist is not self-descriptive nor am I a bigamist,
  Consequently, this defense is that I actually exist!

As an adventurous bridge-builder, I do take risks,
    Uncertainty a natural quality as a "characteristic."
Now Rosling takes emotions apart in statistics,
    Predicting all can become wealthy and healthiest!

HOW THEN CAN I EXIST?

My own situation is not known to be the wealthiest,
    Why I have usual energy, I am not the healthiest!
Most peers would see me as more a modernationist,
    In the middle bridging those who are extremists!

It is accurate to contrast me as internationalist,
    But I would prefer to be considered a globalist!
My experiences have broadened where I exist,
    My perspectives hopefully broaden and persist!

Definitely, I would not be known as a nihilist,
    Neither are the terms unrealistic surrealist!
Nor is the term descriptive as a communist,
    Moreover, neither as I considered a socialist!

Rosling's concept intrigues me as a "possibilitist!"
    Since I am definitely not seen as a creationist!
Yes, creative is descriptive as an existentialist,
    Being over non-being is my manner to exist!

In contrast, I have appreciation of essentialists,
    The essence of phenomena temporarily persists.
While I possess hope to be considered eternalist,
    This is consistent with becoming a possibilitist!

Confessing that I have not ever been a pacifist,
    I have served in the Air Force as a nuclearist.

Research and Development Command we tested
  Nuclear weapons in the desert and the Pacific.

Let me clarify my confusion—I am not a militarist,
  My energy more beneficially addresses injustice!
Micah 6:6-8 in <u>Old Testament</u> reinforces me by
  "Loving mercy, doing justice, walking humbly with God!"

I can be accused of being detached as an idealist,
  Building on principles to be an applied ethicist.
Showing respect, loving neighbor, doing justice,
  A globalist seeking truth in compassionate service.

Yes, I am a theist better known as a monotheist!
  While I practice Buddhist yoga to stay healthiest.
Of course, these commitments are not as a Deist,
  Neither have I ever been known to be an Atheist!

SEEKING BALANCE

At times these broad interests could be "jugglists!"
  Trying to keep everything in the air but not miss.
My own physical balance is not as a perfectionist,
  In my eighth decade, I try to be an "uprightest!"

In physical exercise, I am generally a moderatist,
  This approach intends to have exercise persists.
My muscles are unimpressive but I am not modest,
  Neither am I the slimmest nor obviously heaviest.

Not a polygamist nor a bigamist but monogamist!
  One wife is my new wife after being a "widowist."
Carol as my key anchor tries to keep me "uprightest!"
  I have fallen flat, but fortunately no broken wrist!

Not an artist and no credential as an impressionist,
  Neither am I a violinist, but I am a so-so pianist!
Nor do I advocate being a brief history creationist,
  Nor would I be a pantheist, instead a modernist!

As stated earlier, my interfaith efforts as inclusivist,
  Rather than rigidly exerting beliefs as exclusivist.
"You do not need to be wrong for me to be right!"
  Nor will I relent when imposed with other beliefs!

Do you now really wonder what I actually IST?
  While these efforts are designed to an explicitist!
Rather than hiding behind skirts as an implicitist!
  Instead you may be oversaturated with polyists!

At times, I have tried to be somewhat a humorist,
  But my best intentions may make you the sleepiest!
Understandably, you may resist as poetry persists,
  Neither you nor I would want to become a nihilist!

TIME TO CEASE AND DESIST?

Have we run out of definite term about an IST?
  Maybe I could consider being one who persists!
Certainly, a characteristic mood is not to resist,
  Instead my existence would be for taking risks.

People would typically not consider me a moralist,
  Rather most would consider me to be an ethicist!
People would not consider my slowness as wittiest,
  Instead they would describe me as a traditionalist.

My poetry is now neither refined nor a primitivist,
  Literary critics consider my poetry as elementalist.

Traditional parameters try to trap me into a mold,
But my style instead is to be seen as privately bold.

Fortunately, my existence cannot be a trappist,
My primitive style is what is seen as a "Jerryist."
You may guess that my efforts to define an "IST!"
Has reached it limits in the world we now exist!

Maybe you have never before dealt with futurist!
My occasional dreams are to become a visualist!
The characteristic of IST eliminates old limitists,
Because my own preference is to be a possibilitist!

This existence as eternalist not reincarnationalist!
My own commitment is to be a faithful trustest!
I do not hope to be seen as a psychological egoist!
Instead, my preference is as a natural humanist!

I do not aspire to be the Godliest nor as nastiest
But hopefully to persist as an optimistic realist!
While dementia may naturally occur as I exist,
Neither Alzheimers that will indefinitely persist!

I hope to recognize loved ones plus the friendliest,
Neither would I wish to be helpless or hopeless.
This poetry has not reached ideas to the fullest,
So my aspiration includes being an inclusivist!

8. INTERACTIVELY

THERAPUETIC PERSPECTIVES

Holiday Seasons are very elating!
We patiently hold on by waiting!

This is time when we are expecting!
Families and Friends are gathering!

Children naturally wait impatiently!
Teenagers act disinterested lately!
Gifts are purchased commercially!
Over-eating adds to be weighty!

This season of joy raises expectations!
Balancing the cold of winter season!
As warm hearts greet in relations!
Honoring others with presentations!

We focus on religious and cultural events!
These occasions may uplift our spirits!
Especially as we receive many gifts!
This season provides many reliefs!

UPPERS AND DOWNERS

For some this experience is joyful
For others may become "less-full"
Going from uppers to downers!
Going from downers to uppers!

Others are facing some despair!
Wondering if anyone else cares!
Perhaps feeling trapped inside
Being held like being wrapped!

A person trapped in depression
May fall back in a regression!
Energy expended by elation!
Is stymied by a down recession!

Significant groups in a population,
  Do not find personal connection!
    May have lost a sense of elation,
      Becoming loners void of relations!

Perhaps you already feel badly
Taking another direction quickly!
  To discover the better way out
    Finding a way to turn about!

Moving from downer to upwardly
  Can be helped by moving forward!
    Turning direction may be hard
      Additional factors may reward!

GAINING MOMENTUM

There can be helpful approaches
  There are professionals as coaches!
    And friends might not be sufficient
      As trained persons are efficient!

Physicians can check you physically,
  May provide medication carefully!
    Wise Physicians make referrals
      To those trained in therapy!

Psychiatrists and Psychologists can offer
  Therapeutic services that are proper
    These approaches can be helpful
      By being trained professionals!

A limited number of trained Clergy
   Provide guidance and spirituality!
      Effective combinations collaborate
         By blending skills that cooperate!

Persistence is certainly essential
   So teamwork reaches full potential
      Family & friends can be supportive
         How to become helpful relatives!

Group therapy is also effective
   Sharing by being interactive!
      Participants express involvement
         That jointly can aid "evolvement!"

HOPE

Hope is not magical!
   Hope is hard to do!
      Hope isn't what you hold
         Hope helps by being bold!

"Hope alone is not enough!"
   Positive thinking contribute!
      Breaking out to become resolute!
         Rather than downward pessimism!

But hope alone is not enough!
   One needs to be personally tough!
      Patiently moving ahead by each step!
         Building momentum and more pep!

"Hope makes us more resilient!"
   Coming back into the present!

Bouncing back and not be spent!
Making your life to be decent!

Patience and meditation may work
By regaining perspectives that help!
Engaging with friends and family
Can gain perspectives more readily!

LEARNING TO HOPE

Hope is learned early in life!
Plus trust from parents and mate!
Hope propels us to pursue our goals!
Building success to be like our models!

Hope is what motivates immigrants!
Leaving family coming to United States
Such a powerful force is very crucial
To achieve success and potentials!

Hope is essential in most religions!
Faith, hope & love support decisions![28]
Hope in reaching the Promised Land![29]
Reinforced by anticipation of Advent!

People do not quit by having hope!
Hope's an ingredient how to cope!
Without hope people may perish!
Making hope what humans cherish!

---

[28] The Bible, I Corinthians 13.
[29] The Bible, Deuteronomy 6: 3,

IS HOPING ENOUGH?

As an advisory, these next verses may become perplexing,
    Venturing into vaguely cloudy scenes may be discouraging.
The next section is based upon life experiences and faith,
    There are not assurances that readers will discover help!

So this advice is a time to consider whether to read ahead,
    We are adventuring to questions science does not answer.
Hopeful perceptions are essential without any assurance,
    Venturing forward is largely out of human experience.

ISMS:

Egoism<>Altruism
Objectivism<>Subjectivism
Conservatism<>Liberalism
Libertarianism<>Socialism

ORIENTATION

While these isms have been touted for centuries, there is a current rebirth,
    They are based upon historical experiences that characterize human worth.
Egoism touts primarily self-interest as the basis for human interactions,
    Objectivism elevates reason as the key central creature of scientific factions.

Conservatism has so many meanings that are influenced by diverse cultures,
    Preserving past values of the powerfully influential old successful practices.

There are favorite targets to shoot at from protective, safeguarded positions.
    Concretely, a brief capsule of each typical viewpoints provide impressions.

LIBERTARIAN POSITION ON GOVERNANCE

ISMs express opinions of the practices of national and global governments,
  From socialism to communalistic communism, to democracy & anarchists.
Governance is inherently designed for purposes to organize social systems,
  The perspectives of individualism intrinsically advocates dome resistance.

Libertarian critiques of governments automatically has tension with codes,
  These collective standards conflict with all anti-regulation types of modes.
Individualistic interests react to any imposition of outside restrictions,
  Constraints are viewed as annoyances that challenge personal positions.

The social contract with society is very scant and intentionally restricted,
  Libertarians are appalled at any regulations as evil thus they are depicted.
Responsibilities to each other in social altruism is considered anathema,
  Rather each person for himself in order to pursue their special agenda.

However, objectivism immediately has tensions with anything subjective,
  This abstract position purports to advance investigations as objective.
Scientific methodologies are based upon empirically-based observations,
  Objectivism has limitations in combining the factual and the spiritual.

ADDITIONAL RELIGIOUS ISMS

Religion presents a controversial topic for people wanting their freedoms,
  Any community programs are quickly seen as facets imposing limitations.
These various movements often are guided by masterful leadership.
  Corporate expressions are not the practices of true Libertarian worship.

Since many religion advance fellowship experiences and social groups,
  Libertarians sense impositions that may cause them to be uneasiness.
Egoism likewise naturally adheres to personal practices in true religion,
  Altruistically agendas impose upon their individual self-preoccupation.

Conservatism may readily endorse traditional doctrines and rituals,
　　Typically, conservative can blend both the ancient religious practices.
Selected history is important that highlights their early founding,
　　Preserving these conventions is the meaning of true conserving.

Each of these isms provides critiques of social cultures and institutions,
　　Evaluative judgments are rendered from a position of human illusions.
Imagining that these perspectives are autonomous from participation,
　　Proponents of perspective assume an external stanch of emancipation.

Each ISM accepts their responsibility for carefully shaping behavior,
　　They nurture new adherents so that their tradition will be superior.
Reinforcing their own positions to advocate is a special responsibility,
　　Continuity is challenging when the new ideologies for future posterity.

ECONOMIC CONTRASTS

Since the livelihood of citizens is crucial for their growth and survival,
　　The distribution of resources is vital because each position has a rival.
Economic realities are the arena where the "rubber meets the road!"
　　Since members of the societies' current well-being and future course.

Libertarians often advance capitalism for distribution by free market,
　　Trusting supply and demand will be allocating products & services.
Advocating that buyers and sellers will arrive at appropriate prices,
　　Regulations by government is quickly seen as outside interferences.

Socialism balances individualism so resources are equitably distributed,
　　There is a broader concern about the common good socially contracted.
Regulations inherently place controls upon incoherent rampant chaos,
　　Evenhandedness is crucial for equitable dispersion of economic resources.

Fair distribution is reinforced by the enlightened views of liberalism,
　　Numerous concerns about facilitating imagination and conservatism.
Views varies widely about assumptions of human needs and abilities,
　　Altruism encourages concern for neighbor so that all have possibilities.

ECONOMISTS AND POLITICISTS

In the known history of political economies,
Capitalism and Communism have vied for prominence!
Both have excesses that are issues in rebellions and conflicts.

Related "ists" involve socialists & communists,
The Cold War polarized & dominated 20th century last half.
Capitalists and communists still exist! Ideologies just persist!

Bolshevists are revolutionists wanted power,
Atheism and godless proponents promoted denialists,
Revolutions and elections highlighted these as divisionists!

Leninists advanced Marxism and Maoism
Contrasted with Stalinism and other radicalisms.
Political revolution form hybrids as accommodationists.

Political contests involve idealists and also pragmatists!
Plus conservatism, progressivism and romanticism!
Deists dominated American Constitutional colonialists!

Pessimists have discouraging future outlooks,
They are hopeless when they evaluate predictionists.
Typically they are opposed to optimists who are not shook!

SCIENTISM

Scientists and technologists are readily engaged
In competitive struggles among what researchers studied.
Cosmologists, physicists and anthropologists also vied!

Biologists and geneticists address evolutionists,
Challenged intelligent designists, literalists and Biblicists!
Jurists' trials had difficulty to find solutions as pragmatist.

Socialists seek to understand cross-culturalism,
Psychologists research to discover universal models,
Futurists speculate about universalist and planetarinist!

Evolutionists address changes as naturalists.
Intelligent designists are notorious very brief historicists!
Modernists vs. traditionalists challenge biological geneticists.

Some scientists disbelieve in the divine figures.
Some are atheists but with dedication to scientism.
As naturalism is distinguished from recognizing religion.

MAD TO MAP

We all are familiar with these two words since early grade school,
Mad typically refers to an angry emotion that is seen as hostile!
Map is also well known from our days about studying Geography,
Maps are essential to finding our way around in country and city!

For 50 years, the acronym MAD has acquired another meaning,
During the peak of the Cold War, it referred to mutual bombing!
So the term MAD refers to MUTUALLY ASSURED DESTRUCTION!
Because the Soviet Union and United States used deterrence!

Each polarized superpower possessed arsenals of nuclear bombs,
If one started to bomb the other, retaliation would then be prompt!
Both had capacities to destroy the key targets carried by missiles,
There was no effective defense to protect one from the other!

MAD was considered a rational defense because each understood,
If one launched a preemptory attack, then the other could respond!
The fear inherent in these strategies is ominous to comprehend,
Hopefully these national authorities would be totally rational!

This Nuclear Age resulted in a respectful standoff avoidance,
Decision makers had control and command for offense and defense.
National policies were designed perpetuating this awesome rationale,
Contingent upon an attack from a known source who could launch!

Obviously, flaws were recognized in time revealing vulnerabilities,
If non-nationals obtained access to such weapons caused worries.
If irresponsible nuclear terrorists might hold the world hostage,
If they were not detected, humanity was helpless in this race!

Then serious misunderstandings were discovered with authorities,
President Reagan naively assumed missiles could be recalled!
He apparently made a parallel with recalling airplanes in flight,
Lacking comprehension of irretrievable missiles was set aright!

Another threat was not widely known except by experienced persons,
There is a continuous need to repair and train custodial monitors.
Moreover, as this nuclear weapons became older then another flaw,
Accidental firing could occur due to several flaws in awareness!

One vulnerable feature is that as missiles and bombs begin to age,
Constant attention is essential to repair in order to avoid accidents.
Moreover, deterioration of equipment is a very continuous concern,
Unintended launching ominously threatens creation and humans.

RELIGIONISTS

Pharaonic religions were developed by Egyptians.
Re became the sun god plus Isis the female goddess!
Successive Pharaohs assume the status of deity by people.

Religionists have fought heretics and purists
Dogmatists vs. revisionists vs. modernists vs. anarchists
Have tried literal Donatists plus Nominalists and Arianists!

Reformists battle traditionalists and Papists,
　　Radicalism for purists is nihilistic and ridiculists!
　　　　Soteriologists vie with humanists hold to doctrinalists!

Puritanism object to accommodationists,
　　Plus revivalists, evangelists and also universalists!
　　　　Catholicist challenge Orthodoxist, Montanist and Monists!

Religions with creedalism seek to persist,
　　Who are known as ritualists and also spiritualists!
　　　　Jewish and Islamists experience also challenge novices.

Symbolicists make attempts to convey truth,
　　Many are considered mysticists who remain aloof!
　　　　They prefer myths to truth rather than concrete realists!

　　Cultists headed by extremists recruit loyalists,
　　Who exist for short periods like radical apocalypists!
　　　　Dispensationalists' beliefs in 1000 years for significance!

　　Islamism has spun off in several directions!
　　Early separationists formed Shiites and Sunnis!
　　　　These conflicts continue in identifying issues.

In this century, Fundamentalist Wahhabis,
Mahadists and Qutbists have sprung to action.
　　Wahhabis in Arabia, Pakistan Mahadists, Qutbists in Egypt!

More recently, Madaroists have separated,
Bin Ladism has become anti-West in Afghanistan,
　　Militants jihadists express antagonism to materialism!

LANGUAGE USE AND ABUSE

Language results from highly refined animal and human capacities,
  Non-verbal behaviors communicate a great deal with uncertainties!
For example, in South India, when people turn heads back and forth,
  In Western cultures mean no, but to South Indians this is to affirm!

Traveling in different cultures, nonverbal and verbal is a challenge,
  Long-standing customs are often different from native practices!
Asians and African cultures uniquely communicate with their bodies,
  Westerners may not grasp gestures, attractions or what is naughty.

American students studying abroad benefit from timely preparation,
  Cultural patterns in oral and non-verbal language for communication.
Favorite words and actions can convey very different connotations,
  Global communications have facilitated elementary preparations.

Many persons learn cultural proverbs early plus religious messages,
  Quickly children are influenced by favorite stories, verses and passages.
Puzzling consternation happens when these are examined thoroughly,
  Personal understanding and original meaning intentions symbolically.

A personal demonstration widely known may involve double-checking!
  The story of Jonah and the Whale lends itself to numerous meanings.
Big fish were better known to Hebrews than knowledge about whales!
  Monstrous beings may mean escaping, punishment and even Hades!

Accounts of the Exodus from Egypt by Israelites has many meanings,
  Deliverance is often considered plus magical or miraculous escaping.
Christians have wide interpretations of the "Last Supper" sacramentally,
  Non-believers have considered this an occasion for a drunken party.

Each culture and religious traditions have unique favorite practices,
  These long known ceremonies often are differentially interpreted.
Oral traditions try to provide faithful to origins but are they really?
  How can assumptions of literal translations be known accurately?

Do Christian literalists actually have an understanding of linguistics?
Are currents preachers practicing accurate Biblical hermeneutics?
How might listeners process exactly what is being now transmitted?
Why is the _Quran_ considered definitive in Arabic when it is read?

Many transmitters and translators attempt to doing work accurately,
Are there human limitations in neurotransmitters done verbally?
Does not each person subjectively have their individual perceptions?
When human confusion occurs, do people rely on approximations?

One research demonstration place people in a circular formation,
Experimenters whisper a short account for successive transmission.
In turn, a receiver whispers their account in their communication,
The last recipient then orally relays out loud their comprehension.

Try to guess what transpires in relaying on to the next person?
Do subjective factors naturally amend what they try in recitation?
Typically, after ten persons transmit what they try to remember,
So the last person tells a very different account from the original!

Consider what typically occurs over weeks, months, years & decades,
Do you begin to understand problems in conveying precise passages?
Most ancient stories were relayed through many successive generations,
So that accuracy is declining due to time lags and human limitations!

WRITTEN DOCUMENTS:

Can copied documents convey originals with total precise accuracy?
What are the limits of hand-copied accounts occurred typically?
Even when using just one language does slippage occur noticeably,
Human skills may be polished but will be conveyed practically?

When language is grammatically incorrect in a document originally,
Skillful secretaries will make editorial corrections appropriately.
What is known as "redacting" is designed to improve the grammar,
Careful scholars often make "redactions" as they are professionals.

Human beings have problems in translating into a different language,
Various languages may not have exact work for word counterparts.
Translators attempt to provide reliably freshly conveyed renditions,
They realize that total literal accuracy remains a major question!

Consider printers and copy technology for reproduction,
These are accurate in making copies for wide distribution.
Do editors have preferences in the written languages?
They are extremely reliable as readers have wide variations.

Errors occur that are passed on for future readers and for generations,
Problems obviously happen as documents go through translations.
Languages do not always have counter words with same meanings,
Because translations are not completely reliable when conveying.

Hindu sacred scriptures are recorded in numerous languages of India,
"Urdu" is used in South Asia, but there are understandable slippage.
Hebrew is one of the languages for the Old Testaments literature,
While origins of Hebrew may be a hybrid of Babylonian and Egyptian.

The Old Testament books are also recorded in "The Septuagint!"
This Koinnai Greek is a vernacular while not in classical Greek.
While considerable concurrence is evidence that are variations,
Plus original accounts were orally transmitted by generations.

Muslims insist the Quran is accurately conveyed in Arabic language,
While relying on oral transmission by Mohammed to his own wife.
Plus the assumption that Allah's communication through Gabriel,
This literal dictation to Mohammed was conveyed very precisely!

New Testament gospels, letters and epistles were also written
Greek, Aramaic and Semitic languages were not forbidden.
Collating these various accounts also over decades of time,
Indicates that totally literal accounts are likely imagined.

EXAMINING ASSUMPTIONS:

Literalists make assumptions to be unquestioned or challenged,
*   Denying numerous problems in transmitting through languages.*
They also assume that translators have few human limitations,
*   Convinced that "Divine" preservation is historically provided.*

Contemporary linguistic analyses have carefully found evidence,
*   That multiple authorship is also detectable by different writers,*
The Priestly(P) account, the Elohim(E) and the Yahweh(J),
*   Have convinced careful scholars that accounts widely vary.*

Contemporary science has offered the Quantum factor involved,
*   When actual material is analyzed, it inherently instantly changes.*
Questions naturally arise about the mysteries of investigations,
*   What humans do with subjective propensities and limitations.*

Human communication is advancing collective consciousness,
*   While also discovering that human assumptions lack evidence.*
Wooden regulations of literal accuracy denies human errors,
*   Upon examination of Dogma and Doctrines with less rigor.*

Historically, evidence has been discovered of Scriptural selectivity,
*   St. Paul in his letters took Hebrew Scriptures to then use partially.*
He would select passages he utilized to provide historical precedence,
*   Brian McLaren[30] clearly provides evidence and also scholar's evidence.*

Contemporary "proof-texting" is widely practiced for justifications,
*   Assuming special words out of context have future ramifications.*
This practice is widely abused for authoritative accounts of positions,
*   Not comprehending original contexts or meanings of symbolism.*

"Using Scriptures as Proof-texts" is an attempt for justification,
*   Often strange positions are based upon fallacies in interpretations.*
Sometimes it is possible to distort historical accounts to be supportive,
*   Justifying bizarre prophetic scenarios filled with uncanny positions.*

30

This type of "de-selecting" also occurs deliberately in translations,
   Intimidating positions are used to bolster Scriptural authorities.
Recognizing that many cultures have assumed to be exceptional,
   Makes one cautious in believing authenticity for justification.

Cultural assumptions of "Choseness" needs careful examination,
   Many cultures assume to be the center of the creation's universe.
Radical provincialism and xenophobia are manifestations realized,
   By attempting to justify special uniqueness in order to be prized.

Unsubstantiated beliefs often occur due to much that is unknown,
   Many wise persons admit that there is a great deal not known.
Experienced investigators in many fields respect uncertainties,
   Recognizing creation is so vastly complex there are mysteries!

Possessing openness to discoveries that challenge assumptions,
   Provides a sense of humility to balance human presumptions.
As human beings we are limited, temporary and egocentric,
   Needing counter-balances to realize humans are not magic.

Humble demeanor may counter self-centered pre-occupations,
   Realizing our limitations as creatures in great mysteriousness.
Provincialism and rampant individualism present many problems,
   Balanced by a sense of purpose adding collective consciousness.

III. INTER-PERSONALLY:

9. EDUCATIONALLY

Antitheists hold to exceptionalism in globalism,
These believe their "choseness" beliefs as royalists!
Zionists exemplify they are God's special chosen ones.
Globalism now spawns new forms of "isms and ists!
Nationalism and regionalism advance special interests!
Tribalism and statists are challenged to develop worldviews!

Developmentalists as economists are specialists,
Searching for cohesiveness among those who resist!
Monetarists search for common currencies for mercantilism.

Space travel prompts research for other cultures
and whether they have similar religions and sciences.
The unknown future awaits expanding our earthly perspectives!

Alarmists resist changes in the universe,
Relativists see creation but question physicists!
Open-ended pluralists try to incorporate diverse expansionists!

PERSONAL AND SOCIAL ETHICS

There are wide variations about the values of human beings & creation,
Collective fairness proposes that ethical justice influences all decisions.
When conflicts occur between personal agendas contrasting with society,
Essential are principles in having common understand for consistency.

Comprehensive legal systems are vital for distributive and legal justice,
Access to mediators to do dispute resolution is certainly a social plus.
Justice systems assume the federal, state and global courts are in place,
Cultural values, religion, education & philosophies all could interact.

The whole society is affected by the vectors that influences social ethics,
  Continuous education facilitates how all ages can be community critics.
The quality of life in various nations is affected by human rights & civility,
  Consequently, there are tangible and intangible factors like integrity.

Trustworthiness is an intangible quality in human exchanges in society,
  When trust develops over mistrust, people can function appropriately.
The benefits of conflicting ISMs enrich current and future planning,
  Because people may have trustful confidence that they are growing.

While politics, sex and religion are considered by many to be taboo,
  All of these interactions affect what we, as citizens, are able to do.
Every citizen is affected by political developments in their society,
  Ignoring or avoiding the political arena is less than real propriety!

Yes, politics are messy with conflicts and many different interests,
  There are eager people who would be ready to handle differences.
If there are autocratic leaders, they may wield too much authority,
  If their country has a democratic system, action is taken politically.

IS FREEDOM A MYTH?

Freedom is frequently the American rally slogan!
  Since the Revolutionary War and U.S. Constitution!
    To be free is contrasted to slavery and control by power!

Freedom of the press is touted for a liberated country,
  Protected by the Constitution & courts is a mythology!
    Press media is beholden to corporate interests selfishly!

The press is seen in democracy as the Fourth Estate!
  Holding the three branches of government accountable!
    While corporations use the press to promote interests!

Independence of media is countered by vested power!
  Consequently, "freedom" is bought to be promotional!
    The ideals of the free press are not currently available!

FREEDOM OF RELIGION

To counter the imposition upon all to a state religion,
Constitution writers properly assured religious freedom!
Government is not to establish or interfere with religion!

This dual provision permits persons to make choices,
Exercising their convictions without government voices!
This experiment in religious freedom is worthy to evaluate!

Mainline religions do not consistently honor free choice!
Both families and sub-cultures indoctrinate for allegiance!
Religion is often inherited through teaching & nurturance!

Clergy support religious freedom but within constraints!
Economically beholden to their institution's resources!
Few clergy are prophetically independent as free voices!

Individual freedom of religious choice is being threatened!
Subtle influence is conveyed in the market and government!
Deliberate attention essentially protects what is essence!

POLITICAL FREEDOM

Freedom to vote as a citizen is a prize of democracy!
Both voting and seeking office is possible for citizenry!
These provisions are inherently attractive possibilities!

Of course, special interests of parties exert influence!
Coalitions form pursuing agendas and special persistence!
Campaigns are competitive while candidates seek office!

There are typically expenditures made by candidates!
But recently inordinate funding is considered legitimate!
Consequently wealthy interests have inordinate influence!

Fair elections have an ideal of "one person, one vote!"
Enormous contributions reduce personal significance!
Free elections succumb to winning due to rich plutocrats!

Democracy is being threatened again by special interests!
Influencing elections plus efforts to control governments!
Both oligarchies and autocracies dangers are imminent!

ECONOMIC FREEDOM

Free markets are prized by powerful commercial practices,
Balance in these markets by "The Invisible Hand of God!"
Adam Smith[31] advocated the myth as business was small!

Supposedly the distribution of economic resources is wide,
But concentrations of money are spent by big corporations!
A sense of divine equilibrium is more a myth not realized!

Fair distribution among persons is not being realized,
Great Recessions occur in this economy and worldwide!
Powerful structures now largely shape how we distribute!

Free market is a euphemism by being controlled by wealthy,
Enlightened self-interest by Reagan-Bushes in Presidencies!
They did not recognize a Great Recession in the economy!

The free market advocates contradict their own advocacy!
Banks and Financial Corporations seek government rescue!
Free market economics only what they control with power!

Powerful wealthy are protected while workers suffer,
The free market myth is primarily for those with power!
Inequitable distribution of resources has a limited future!

---

[31]   Smith, Adam

When special interests try to dominate resource distribution,
Human development and growth are being also threatened!
Conscientious protectors of freedom are a requirement!

Is free market economics America's transactional religion?
"Free" has appealing ring when looking for a transaction!
"Market" suggests a smorgasbord of foods and nutrition!

The "blood" of American economy is money accumulation!
On the open market is a variety of stock, bonds and products;
"Retail Therapy and Prosperity Theology" are on markets!

Buying a ticket to heaven is almost explicitly merchandised!
Even more appealing is a return trip to check the Dow Jones!
But not as a rather major stretch of God's Invisible Hands?

NEED TO DISCOVER EQUAL BALANCE

Human experiences are inherently expressed paradoxically,
Polarities include male-female, good-evil and human-Divine!
These features are balanced by its inherent polar opposite!

Emphasis on one pole ignores its other counterpart,
Humanity is beginning to acknowledge gender balance,
Both masculine-feminine and human-Divine are essential!

One-sided freedom is out of balance without duties!
Freedom also has to be countered by responsibilities!
Free markets are wishful thinking without obligations!

The current economic theories identify two polarities:
Capitalism has motivated to be "Extract" global resources!
The polar balance is to be inclusive rather than exclusive!

Capitalism requires extracting that leads to disparities,
The rich extract wealth at the expense of those in poverty!
Involvement of governments helps protect the vulnerable!

Adam Smith's "Invisible Hand" had cohesive community;
Not rampant individualism that is emphasized currently.
Resource distribution of God's creation is for all humanity!

Religions and political freedom likewise needs balance,
Our freedom of the press calls for balanced coverage!
Humanity always finds equilibrium by faith in the Divine!

USING-FAITHING-CONCEDING-ADORING-IDOLIZING!

Has the Free Market become the secular Western god?
Americans express trust blindly in this economic idol!
While business and banking leaders worship this god!

Many American economists may be losing their balance!
Straw men are created in the thinking of decision-makers!
Communism clearly opposed capitalism as its challenger!

A misinterpreted straw man is our degrading socialism!
Do we limited human beings create advantages selfishly?
Consuming the vulnerable for our appetites unknowingly?

In collective corporate decision-making, do we exploit?
Assuming powerful wealth partials out resources for us?
By disguising our propensities to take all that we can get?

Is "The Invisible Hand" now made our handmaiden?
How long will we be deceived by our own creations?
Permitting us to cover-up self-interests as forbidden?

Establishing ourselves with all-knowing pretensions?
Justifying our actions as the preference for humanity?
While ignoring all innocents victims in our chess play?

Wealthy royalty and others, we have pawns and subjects?
Not considering them as valued persons but as objects?
Unconscious abuse of power is really exerted with hubris!

As if others in creation can be used for our purposes?
Blindness can infringe on our judgment on ourselves!
So that we might be unaware how we are really selfish?

These are not questions to comfort but to disturb us!
Trying to fathom how chronically we are self-possessed!
Hopefully our reflections may balance how we are messed!

FROM FEAR THRU FORTITUDE
TO FREEDOM

Human challenges in search of freedom are so inherently inspiring,
Aung San Suu Kyi's tells that she is "free in un-free" Burma living![32]
She personally discloses her inner strength for finding inner peace!
Hoping that the terribly vicious attacks would eventually cease.

As a contemporary heroine, Aung reveals her own personal secrets,
These are uniquely her own, confirming experiences history shows.
In her native Burma, her special gifts for writing were stymied,
Fortunately, her formidable fortitude has helped Aung to survive!

Her "cowshed" now is headquarters for National League for Democracy,
Reflects her recognition of the humble birth of Jesus, not aristocracy.
Along with Gandhi and Martin Luther King, Aung reflects simplicity,
These pioneers of freedom like Lincoln inspired us to seek our liberty!

---

[32] "One woman's inner strength," July 11, 2011, <u>The Christian Science Monitor</u>

As a woman, she demonstrates that physical prowess is not essential,
 Like historical heroines, her humbleness contradicts military militias.
Aung exemplifies the power of physical powerlessness for might,
 External muscles mislead traditional assumptions of what is right!

Ironically the "Power History" tends to suggest a necessary strength,
 This fails to recognize the innate and inner power revealed at length.
The Beatitudes[33] challenge human assumptions of traditional power,
 "The meek shall inherit the earth" contradicts the need for fighters.

Yes, "fighters" are composed of a wide range for admirable assets.
 For healing to progress, a "fighting attitude" can defeat setbacks.
Puzzled surgeons concerned with their patient's capacity to fight,
 Because they hope to work with the patient's own "fighting spirit!"

CONVERTING ANXIETY TO SPECIFIC FEARS

"Free-floating anxiety" haunts many people at times into paralysis,
 Anxious persons can become immobilized to feel almost helpless.
Because many do not sense what is prompting their restlessness,
 They are therapeutically assisted with special tested techniques.

Therapists make efforts to discover these anxieties in psychotherapy,
 Trustful relations that are confidential help to discover some remedy.
One of a number of strategies involves converting anxiety into fear,
 Because free-floating anxiousness is difficult to combat or to fight.

When anxiety is unspecified, a client does not recognize what to fight,
 Efforts to identify what prompts anxiety create targets in one's sight.
That is why pervasive anxiety is so ominous for persons to combat.
 More specific targets are more readily combated as a real subject.

---

[33]   Matthew 5: 5-12 in the "New Testament" of the Bible.

With specified causes are identified, both client and therapists work,
   To develop strategies to ameliorate the uneasiness that may thwart,
When targets are identified, focused efforts are much more effective,
   Otherwise, a client is struggling with unknown nightmares of fright.

Giving clients medications is only partially effective in this process,
   This "quick-fix" approach fails to recognize the causes of distress.
In fact, medications can reduce capacities to solve their problems,
   Without problem-solving strategies, the client is stuck into space.

When clients actively combat "targeted fears" they gain confidence,
   In their own personal capacities to cope with their own reticence.
Practice, support, practice, praise, practice, support and so forth,
   The art of therapy is a challenge to be patient with one's patients!

Once persons gain competence coping with their own anxiousness,
   Transferring this skill needs cultivating as challenges are different.
Then an empirically validated discovery assists in more coaching,
   Moderate anxiety is then optimal for curvilinear problem solving!

If anxiety is too high, panic may stymie positive responses to cope,
   If anxiety it too low, then typical persons could be unresponsive.
Moderate anxiety can be both motivating and prompt peak behavior,
   With experience more in problem-solving, clients learn to discover.

Overall strategy converts free-floating anxiety into defined fears,
   Then persons have a target as their enemy with him to conquer.
Specific sets of targets are the focus of new problem solving skills,
   Concentrating strategies of coping help changing anxiety to fears.

Many people do not understand that fear is also a survival strategies,
   Without defensive fears, people are vulnerable to many tragedies.
Specific fears are considered a protective mechanism of survival,
   Without alertness to pending disasters, the person is vulnerable.

PREAMBLE

Blessings on our American Founding Fathers who fought for freedoms,
  They exemplified both responsibility & rights of freedom for us humans!"
They personally faced repression by oppressive authorities firsthand,
  Little might they have realized the paradoxical truths of their demands.

They had numerous reasons to fight for freedoms to resist oppression,
  Like humanity for millennia, they had limits to their free expression.
When a toddler is taken out of their playpen they are free to explore,
  But they need to be watched carefully least they escape out the door!

When these "freedom fighters" fought for what they considered right,
  Did they realize the imbalance in their emphases on championing fright?
Did they have awareness that there are paradoxical truths to behold?
  Were they not responsible for leading the American Revolution so bold?

America has touted to be the "Land of the Free and Home of the Brave!"
  These slogans mobilize American people who readily break into a rave.
So the following balance may not be readily understood by the patriots,
  In fact, many Americans who do not readily reflect see this as outcasts?

Does not the privilege of the rights of freedom also infer a clear balance?
  Do not "Freedom Riders" inherently feel motivated to express experience?
Can you sense that insistence upon one truth does not address reactions,
  Addressing this imbalance can create counter forces into brutal factions.

Those of us who defended our national freedoms from external threats,
  Are at least eligible to express concerns while also covering our own bets.
Military service is designed to protect America from external enemies,
  But might we recognize a weakness in our own honored transparencies?

Yes, we are "Freedom Fighters" who are willing to make our sacrifice,
  Does that infer that from serving in our country we are blind to balance?
We may readily label other defenders of their traditional propensities,
  Do these claims excuse us from identifying our more marginal issues?

Our reservations that as humans we have both objectivity and balance,
Might these also be jeopardized by our vested interest or clear readiness?
Are we ready to address the tough issues about "Rights & Responsibility!"
Or "collolaries" usually labeled as Democratic Party Platform propensity?

CREATION DILEMMAS

Often we emphasize one aspect of our generous freedoms from Creator,
Who may wonder how we free creatures handle these in our incubator.
Our Creator can be accused of taking many risks for being responsible,
Our Foundation for living in earth could also be recognizes as flexible.

So what are the balances on freedom to choose and rights to also decide?
Be patient as together we explore this complex mystery of living outside!
We're not confined by restrictions while Genesis suggests few guidelines,
"Be fruitful and multiply!" are commands for us to live in "His Space!"

Blessed with Time and Space to exercise our inherent human freedom,
Our Creator may have pondered how we would handle His Kingdom!
So can you imagine what happens as we experience these free rights?
Probably parallel humans would create their children with some frights.

Who are surprised humans quickly emphasized one side of equation?
Historical and mythical accounts report humans are full of evasion!
We blame the "Snake" as a mythological account of responsibility,
Eve did blame this seductive crawling creature for being a liability.

Do we as evasive creatures learn how to shift our responsibilities?
And do we project our inherent incapacities onto other personalities?
Perhaps we might recognize our propensities to express our denials,
Like pleading "Not Guilty," a protected freedom at our own trials?

Do we as human beings have our rationalizations for our excuses?
Might we ever acknowledge our human weaknesses that seduces?
"Shifting Responsibilities" onto external sources is now known,
With a minor child this is acceptable but how about its parent?

Adults who shift responsibilities by then blaming someone else,
　　Are conspicuous to others but may not be an insight themselves.
Adults are assumed to be wiser than children without experience,
　　Who has known adults who are still living in childhood existence?

Being evasive, we become likely we likely project responsibilities,
　　It is known as "Shifting Responsibilities" instead of "Obligatories."
This is an insidious defense mechanism that helps us to evade,
　　Being held accountable for what adults are expected to pervade.

Some label this tendency as our practicing "Placing the Blame;"
　　So often we are so evasive that we do not experience full Shame.
Adults are expected to be accountable while we overlook a child,
　　Are adults all really grown up or are there those who are wild?

Could we have learned from parents to be evading as a right?
　　If so, this perpetuates irresponsibility into future with fright.
Could leaders in high places also be leading in blame placing?
　　Since a whole culture be caught into the snare of displacing?

Take both our heritage of the free and our religious freedom,
　　Is this what the Divine contemplated for ruling His Kingdom?
Did our Creator expect us to be both creative and responsible?
　　Or was Our Creator providing excuses to be so irresponsible?

While human parents often expect teenagers to be dependable,
　　Can our Creator assume we as adults can make this expendable?
Rarely do we find adults who accept lame our childish excuses,
　　Instead, adults are expected to fully our handle responsibilities.

Implications are numerous in daily living and in our democracy,
　　Even our constitution overstates an imbalance in name of liberty.
Our Creator likely assumes His Experiment in this Universe,
　　Will act more authentically than those who have no converse.

How might Our Creator view our human propensities to deny?
　　Is Our Creator to tolerate our foibles instead of us willing to try?
Can Our Creator consider as an excuse to forgive our immaturity?
　　Can our own Creator accept that High Divinity is ready for Duty?

HUMAN DILEMMAS

Now let us apply these realizations to issues that face humanity,
Even personally, nationally and globally, our problems are plenty.
How are our propensities to engage in shifting our responsibility,
Acceptable on this globe as well as understandable to Divinity?

These penetrating questions are issues needing our own attention,
These issues may be evadable but leave us with human pretension.
Are we "Blame Placers" who project responsibilities onto others?
Are we mature in our roles as adults where not mother smothers?

Did our parents or teachers advise us when a bully acted out;
"Just ignore him" so that he does not get attention to shout?
This advice was given by our top national leaders in lurch,
When Rev. Jones burned <u>Qurans</u> at his Florida Church.

"Just ignore him" was not effective in dampening him down,
Jones excessive needs for attention make him even a clown.
Exercising his freedoms like a circus clown can do for laughs,
This Pastor again acted foolishly but not for more gaffes.

Over one dozen innocent public servants were kills in revenge,
In Afghanistan, other extremists reacted to action by Jones.
American Freedoms did not implore him to act responsibly,
He wanted attention out of irresponsible passion publicly.

<u>A Biblical</u> issue from the creation myth of Adam and Eve,
Did Adam ever say to Eve: "Just ignore the snake please!"
Perhaps Adam did not know what to say or was ignorant,
Does this explain humanities so-called simple innocence?

God-given freedom to make our choices as free creatures,
Great risk of creating humans with trust in our features.
Does this excuse Jones or humanity from responsibilities?
Does this exemplify how limited fragile our sensibilities?

RATIONALIZATIONS

Do Americans hide behind Constitutional freedom skirts?
　　Knowing we are not mature in exercising what we exert?
Free rights and social responsibility are difficult to manage,
　　We have much to learn in our immature human image.

Parental models have had limitations we have all inherited,
　　We cannot blame them for realities their parents projected.
Simultaneously, we're lead by political leaders who are human,
　　They do not have Divine insights to guide them in decisions.

In human society, there are numerous models who place blame,
　　Onto others rather than they themselves accepting shame.
Both sides have extremists projecting onto others externally,
　　The deflectors serve protective roles to evade responsibility.

Each culture has traditional enemies, who are readily blamed,
　　Anyone in that culture who is not loyal is also then shamed.
Human protective mechanisms are powerful to serve our need,
　　So denial is among many ways to protect us as we proceed.

Yes, in each antagonistic nation there are patriotic minorities,
　　These readily become extremists who react to any attack,
They imagine they are protecting their heritage from outside,
　　Often they are not aware of global issues and their picture.

So natural rivals have built-in defenders who resist any attack,
　　They are the first to respond so they almost act as a pack.
Whenever any negative occurs in the new or in global rumor,
　　These extremists react very defensively without any humor.

They are serious and deadly in their venom against enemies,
　　These elements are so sensitized to react very defensively.
So readily the rival nations create their own enemy attackers,
　　Their own comrades are influenced to be staunch Backers.

So when there are naïve attacks posted by media of the enemy,
    The defenders react into the world media very immediately.
Should others be surprised when these reactions are reported?
    Can't they grasp opponents cheer their own as supported?

Into this inflammatory global scene are reports of extremists,
    These are fanatics who are now threatened by any resistance.
How can the explosive situations be calmed from extremities?
    A major challenge to "responsible defenders of freedoms!"

Extremists are present on all sides of our human divisions,
    These irresponsible extremists challenge our own decisions.
Balancing judgment is very difficult for subjective humans,
    Our own vested interests take precedence in our relations.

The hard paradoxes involved in Rights vs. Responsibilities,
    Also show up in issues of Freedoms vs. Social Obligations.
Do humans have duties when we exercise our free choices?
    Or do we act entirely in our decisions as free individuals?

COURAGEOUS FORTITUDE

All living creatures benefit from encountering life as challenges,
    Each being is strengthened when learning skills and alliances.
The fearless creatures are the prey of their aggressive enemies,
    In watching animals and birds, their defenses reveal alertness!

Nature is inherently practicing survival by the most competent,
    To cope with challenges requires genetic and learned talents.
With practiced skills in both defensive and offensive procedures,
    Creatures gain capacities to adapt and learn new competencies.

Courage is a learned skill dealing with challenging environments,
    The confident young and seniors display why their competence.

Without capacities for risky adventures, this species is threatened,
Trial and error plus more powerful modeling can also be learned.

Persons with tested confidence know the strengths and weaknesses.
Learning what is successful and also the maladaptive behaviors.
The most successful in skill building learn taking calculated risks,
Defeats, setbacks and even injuries all contribute to being brisk!

Bravery can be helpful or foolish in order to survive testy situations,
Without experimentation, very few creatures cope with conditions.
Courageous fortitude is re-enforced with successes and failures,
When brave experimenters try next steps, they also know lures.

Fortitude engenders inner strengths that contribute to competency,
The steadfast new anchors of support reduce fear and also anxiety.
Creatures in new experiences are essential for "faith, hope and love,"
Trust in one's Maker and one's skillfulness takes us in adventures.

It is not just alpha males or attractive females who are vulnerable,
But the middle levelers who are less stressed more than weakest.
Foolish risks are inherently recognized by surviving brains & brawn,
Calculated skills are strengthened with each successful new plan.

FREEDOM FROM WHAT FOR WHAT?

This question provokes multiple responses as variables to know,
Freedom is composed of colorful facets that are like a rainbow.
Freedom is relative to other factors depending on your containers,
Within this box is one of many freedoms; without many dangers!

Internal freedom is primarily perceptions of one's mind over time,
External to one's body, are open spaces and boundaries sublime.
Functioning within one's personal frame varies from one another,
Within a family, freedom may be different from sister to brother.

"She's a free lassie!" "He's stuck on himself!" are differentiations,
  Individual variations are so vast so any two are distinct persons.
We may consider "degrees of freedom" as statistical variations,
  In contrast, one's internal private life can have deep foundations.

First, are personal experiences that are unique to an individual,
  No two have precisely experiences that will ever be identical.
A person's frame of reference has many dimension that happen,
  People are exclusively themselves so vary in their own freedom.

Secondly, a person has unique physical features like no one else,
  Even everyone face has distinctiveness about how we recognize.
While, we all have 99% similar genetic composition we share,
  Our special one percent composes our internal special sphere.

Thirdly, each person is socially special in how we know our freedom,
  Aung is like no one else in Burma as we are different in our home.
Our civil freedom depends upon our culture plus our own learning,
  Both nature and nurture influence our identity in our socializing.

Next, we are each living in the dimensions of space and of time,
  Economically we have assets and liabilities that cause us to rhyme.
Politically our nationality will have various "degrees of freedom,"
  From wide latitude for actions to constraints under regulations.

"Freedom and responsibility" are paradoxically connected for each,
  We may focus on "either-or polarities" not seeing how to connect.
Young have fewer responsibilities in their freedom than their elders,
  Seniors may feel heavy burdens limiting the ranges as key actors.

Spiritually there are powerful experiences that may vary widely,
  One person's spiritual freedom may very different and uniquely.
Martin Luther discovered in his struggles of life these variations,
  His teachings influence Westerners for over five hundred years.

Drawing on St. Paul's insights in his letter to Christians in Galatia,
Luther grasped these paradoxical relations stated so succinctly:
"We are uniquely free from all constraints that bear upon each one,
In order that we are free to be slave of all," down to each person.

This paradox connects polarized components contained in freedom,
With these multiple facets, we have special relations to everyone.
Trying to escape from these human truths or paradoxical living,
We forego the humanizing experiences that make us civilizing.

FREEDOM FROM FEARS

Our fears can have a paralyzing consequence that is complicated,
Fear is both helpful and harmful when it is not properly managed.
We receive signals in our primitive brains from innate protection,
These involuntary reactions are essential for survival fortification.

If our lives are dominated by primitive fears, human are stymied,
The judgments of higher order decisions need to be conditioned.
When organisms are predominant motivation becomes defensive,
Then creative adventures fail to develop new tactically offenses.

This phenomena is observed when children are afraid to venture,
Overly-protective parents try to rescue children to feel secure.
Children's risk-taking becomes impaired when lives are restricted,
Developing confidence to undertake new skills is then inhibited.

Balance in protective measures with skill development is crucial,
Fear is inherently on guard, but risk-taking is becomes gradual.
Otherwise persons become imprisoned in their cocoon of safety,
Eventually the organism is suffocated by parents acting carefully.

In nurturing creativity, new experiences are keys to be highly valued,
Developing novel remedies to old problems needs to be rewarded.

Calculated risk-taking is essential to balance between two factors,
Learning new skills foster more creative living to face stresses.

An inverted "U" is offered to visualize these abstract conceptions,
This means that linear thinking is better challenges with ideations.
The following page depicts the complex relationships involved,
These insights can help one cope with problems to be solved.

Traps of fearful-living stifle progress, risk-taking and adventures,
This model also suggests that handling fears are learned ventures.
These patterns of behavior have application to persons and nations,
Collective action to cope with fear-engendering enemies is essential.

Balanced decision-making involves handling both cautions and risks,
Individuals learn on a personal level as nations face global tricks.
When fearful persons make decisions for cultural security risking,
Leaders can get overly protective or too risqué in decision-making.

Examples from recent history can be tested with this model,
Applications to national decisions that result in more failure.
Moreover, personal learning is essential to work on teams,
Joint risk-taking decisions can be difficult and still successful.

LABELS NEEDING ANALYSIS

Historical figures illustrate a wide range of overcoming fears,
Brave leaders have addressed crises to help those in futures.
Take Moses who led the Exodus recorded in religious history,
He feared he had limitations that would leave people in misery.

Greek dramas portray how mythical heroes faced challenges,
Hindu mythology describes how figures met fears head-on.
Over-protected Buddha in childhood later developed bravery,
These figures dramatically learned to overcome "fear-slavery!"

The Historical Jesus demonstrated faith that overcomes fears,
  He had inspired people worldwide to take undertake risks!
Gandhi illustrates challenges to traditional military strategy,
  He also pioneered like Jesus how nonviolence needs bravery.

Martin Luther King, Jr., built upon the combined models or old,
  His commitment to nonviolence prompted him to become bold.
Challenging tradition in their cultures resulted in deep resistance,
  Jesus, Gandhi and King were assassinated by opposing fanatics.

In Auschwitz Prison, Viktor Frankl and Mike Jacobs were held,
  As Jewish persons, they coped with Hitler's fanatical fears.
Both of these men survived as did those who handled fear,
  They had hope, energy and meaningful relations that held.

Other prisons of fear are being battled by brave one each day,
  Uniquely these surviving heroes and heroines found their way.
Many overcome "social controllers" who use emotional abuse,
  Others are actually held physically as by traffickers of sex.

Those who held by addictions of drugs, nicotine or of sweets,
  Cope with the dynamics that are physical and psychological.
Addictions is also a chronic habit of consumers out of control,
  They risk economic bankruptcies and ostracism while social.

Modern hi-techies can be addicted to the Internet and phones,
  "Alone-Together" and "Together-Alone" reveal these clones.
Political dictators and economic greed also result in slavery,
  Physical confinement right along with more economic poverty.

Determinism and fate can be advocated so these may imprison,
  Rigid scientists can be trapped in their understanding of reality.
Religious fanatics can be enveloped into their own practices,
  Confining their freedoms to act in strategies as redemptive.

Media are subtle traps when advertising and violence is prized,
   Video games, twitter and Face Book are now not a surprise.
Mental manipulation imposed by outside sources or internally,
   Can imprison addictive safety so that we controlled externally.

However, labeling these general diagnoses does not get at causes,
   Diagnosing problems is essential in order to find real treatments.
Remember, humans can be trapped in fears internally in our brain,
   External imprisonment may not be as obvious as some assume.

10. SCIENTIFICALLY

Experiments in Progress

Tests of capacities for employees to responsibly handle freedom,
   Has been undertaken by employers in a working experiment.
"Ultra-flex Jobs: You Choose Hours and Venues,"[34] is involved.
   Employees arrange their own hours and place for their work.

Freedom to handle responsibilities are researched for results,
   Initially, they have discovered greater employee productivity.
Most workers are fulfilled when they are working successfully.
   Compatible with employers unique needs to meet standards,

Flexibility provides options to how and when employees work,
   This takes responsible professionals and technological persons.
With better performance plus more satisfaction than scheduling,
   These positive measures suggest success in workers producing.

In any experiment with human participants there is subtle impact,
   They recognized confounding variable of the Hawthorne effect.

---

34   Price, Margaret "Ultraflex Jobs: You Coose Hours and Venues," The Christian
     Science Monitor, July 4, 2011

When people know that they are involved in a new experiment,
They typically feel that now they are getting special attention.

This awareness can inflate research results with some artificiality,
People enjoy being uniquely treated then increase productivity.
Inexperienced researchers may fail to note confounding factors,
Further replications of this experiment can verify these actors.

Irrespective of discoveries this experiment is helpfully suggestive,
Challenging other variations in different settings to be objective.
Initially, we can recognize: "From Fear Thru Flexibility to Freedom,"
Expresses initial discoveries that consideration could also affirm.

The current electronic revolutions in communications frees up
Participants who become involved who rapidly know results.
When people have prompt feedback, the better they perform,
Examples are derived from hunting and sports about games.

Astute observers of revolutions in North Africa and Middle East
Are reporting synergistic efforts producing even more results.
While the internet, ipods, cell phones, and twitter are working,
These rapid communications system accelerate those revolting.

These rapid changes during 2011 had amazed the rigid structures,
The participants moved from fear through fortitude onto freedom.
Major risk-taking is inherently involved with lives as the stakes,
Momentarily communicating informs and synergistically inspires.

High technology communication is changing many old practices,
Virtual teamwork can occur both locally and also now globally.
People connect in similar causes, circumstances and concerns,
This can multiply effectiveness elsewhere very instantaneously.

Traditional media is experiencing this radical change in business,
News is decreasingly provided by print media but by broadcast.

A recent film, "Page One," depict changes in leading newspapers;
 The intense pace of sharing information bombards most viewers.

Like development of written language affected consciousness,
 Plus the historical revolution with innovative printing presses.
Electronic communications are radically transforming today,
 Instantaneous communication radically influences us globally.

We are riding the new wave crests that are leaving an imprint,
 Future generations will be affected with results as important.
Human beings with simultaneous communication will change,
 Handling these new developments is a key to our human brains.

Yes, our defensive brains notice signals of anxiety for protection,
 Signaling fears will result in adaptive behaviors of inhibitions.
How rapidly humans can assimilate these current developments,
 Directly will impact now how we undertake our new challenges.

WHAT FORECASTS ARE FEASIBLE?

In order to manage fears, multiple strategies become essential,
 Human beings benefit from learning from risks to find potential.
External controls by subtle mind-control or bodily confinement,
 Plus internal prisons within our own inner fear of adventure.

Creative skills require both learning within and then also without,
 Problem-solving individually and collectively help get us about.
Without keen awareness of these invisible controls is confining,
 Adventurous spirits can liberate their self-imposed restraining.

There are more reasons to hope than to fear in our human living,
 Ancestors provide both what is successful than what is failing.
Posterity depends on our courageous fortitude to face realities,
 These challenges are the agenda for both now and potentialities.

SIGNIFICANT APPROACHES
TO DEVELOPING

Globally, most humans engage in narcissism.
  Naturally, we view the world from our perspectives.
Likewise, we are blessed with our personal universe!
  We see our world through our own perceptiveness!

Conflicts result from diverse personal viewpoints,
  In infancy, we are center of the world of our parents!
They created us as infants who see egocentrically.
  Center of attention, we are readily behave selfishly.

        Wider perspectives encounter conflicting worldviews!
          At first we may assume that the sun and moon follow us!
        Other persons are seen as planets in "my own universe!"
          From "me" to "thee" there are clashes of differences.

Aware of other persons is a major development,
  Incorporating us in their world as supplements!
Early childhood, we may become a complement,
  By six, most capably see the others' viewpoints!

        Brothers and sisters help us to grow up socially,
          Egocentric views are challenged into diversity!
        Classmates and teammates provide experience,
          Our worldviews expand to appreciate the Universe!

Adolescent egocentrism show in very new avenues!
  "Personal fables"[35] try to imagine our own influence!
Conceiving imaginary worlds where we are the focus!
  Assuming our performances seen by wide audiences!

---

[35] Elkind, D., A Sensitive Understanding of Children and Adolescence.

Individual differences fascinate our consciousness,
Consolidating others into our growing awareness!
Natural tensions continue into the multi-Universes,
Learning about others' views is social intelligence!

HISTORICAL DEVELOPMENTS

The Greeks encouraged curiosity about the Universe!
Of course, they had imaginations but without sciences!
Stimulating creative minds expanding their culture,
Nurturing adventures into philosophy and literature!

Theology is concerned with how to arrive in heaven!
But theology does not explain how heaven works!
Egypt's Alexandria promoted lively imaginations,
Mathematics and astronomy led into experiences.

Copernicus had explanations of solar circularity,
Catholics presumed to be arbiter of controversy.
The courage of Copernicus assisted astronomy!
Fostering individual intelligence to change destiny!

Kepler's[36] mathematics verified that planets orbit the sun,
By confirming that earth is not center of the universe!
His calculations merit our own appreciative credit!
Mathematics provides calculations of orbits of planets!

These pioneers of astronomy laid foundations,
Theology knows heaven, not heaven's cosmology,
Newton found gravity as the force holding all!
His elegant experiment has profound discoveries!

---

[36]   Kepler,

Galileo courageously challenged religious authority,
*   In the 20th century, Einstein's relative space and time![37]*
While Hubble's telescope provides more key evidence
*   That this Universe is expanding into outer space!*

Awareness of creation diminishes human significance,
*   We cannot be considered the center of the Universe!*
Appreciating cosmology enlarges more mysteries,
*   Prompting our minds about numerous uncertainties!*

11. RELIGIOUSLY

Our Universe Enlarges

Discovering the world does not rotate around me!
*   Sets the stage for individuals to see other "thous!"*
As our world expands, so do wider appreciations!
*   Reality feedback we are infinitesimal in creation!*

Tribes and nations go through parallel realizations,
*   Ethnocentrism fosters outlooks that "We" are the Chosen!*
Cultures assume that the world rotates around them!
*   This tribal ethnocentrism creates conflicts with many!*

Narrow human thinking can make us look very foolish,
*   While identifying human propensities to be selfish!*
Religions become appropriated to "just my own people!"
*   As if we take the exclusive possession of the deities!*

This dynamic grows from individual egocentrism!
*   Enlarged by my people to become "religio-centric!"*

---

37   Einstein, A.,

Our personal God is just concerned with mine!
Perspectives that ethnic deity has narrowness.

Consider historical examples for data supporting:
Egypt's Sun deity, Re, was theirs with expert priests!
Israelites see themselves as Jehovah's own "Chosen!"
He gives them "The Promised Land" to be exclusive!

Christians have parallel dynamics in the Trinity!
Using these criteria to "test" what others believe!
Persecution and trials determined the heretics' fate!
Non-believers were killed without public confessions!

Muslims encounter these mutually exclusive traditions,
Conflicts can be very violent unless there is toleration!
Islam worships Allah expecting devoted submission,
While Hinduism and Buddhism have more inclusion!

In Old Spain, various religions were historically located,
Jews, Muslims and Christians all studied together!
The Inquisition was intolerant so universities suffered,
Catholic defensively fought Muslims in Middle East!

"Intolerant Religion!" is also strange to be considered,
"The Dangers of Religious Supremacy" is apparent!
It exclusivity occurs, that reaches violent intolerance,
Countering trust, respect, love and inclusive grace!

INTERFAITH EXPERIMENTS

Nations with constitutions honor "religious freedom!"
These labs test whether inclusive over intolerant religion!
Social ethnocentrism is a dynamic to explore inclusion!
These are parallels to egocentrism and cultural narcissism!

Social relations often have major divergent tensions;
  Ethnic tribes and intolerant nations may see enemies!
What might cultivate both tolerance and cooperation?
  Consider other approaches for more experimentation!

Athletics thrive on active sports guided by regulations!
  Greeks pioneered The Olympics for expert competition!
Now in recent centuries, international teams compete,
  Respecting nonviolent referees for great athlete to meet!

Soccer is the primary sport in African and South America,
  Europe's nations vigorously engage for championships.
African nations now experiment with greater cohesion,
  Sports appeal to many people to foster better relations!

Interfaith experiments are pioneering mutual respect!
  Curious participants try openness rather than conflict!
Propensities to be different rather than our similarities,
  Human genes are 99.9% identical with few disparities!

Why do we emphasize differences with other persons?
  Seeing the contrasts we have from sisters and brothers!
Our external appearances are primarily on the surface,
  We strive to be exceptional for personal distinctiveness!

Analogous patterns influence how we see religions.
  Assuming we are unique that emphases differences.
Inferring other beliefs are not equivalent to our own,
  With superior perspectives that discredit unknowns.

Interacting with diverse cultures, helps us to learn,
  We also come to more deeply understand ourselves!
These broadening experiences also have great value,
  Both for ourselves plus diverse peoples whom we know!

Religions hold key relationship as sacred to them,
   The Golden Rule is expressed in various services!
Love is held in common in reciprocal relations,
   Respect and integrity are advocated by religions!

Discovering commonalities is very refreshing,
   What is held together for mutual understanding!
While distinctive beliefs and rituals are practiced,
   Appreciating each other's practices is encouraged!

PREPARING TO DO NEW RESPONSIBILITIES!

CONVERGENCIES:

Participating in Arts by engaging,
   Writing, preparing, revising, editing
      Then publishing, advertising, distributing.

Engaging in Music:
   Singing, playing instruments,
      Composing, practicing and performing!

Sustaining Talents for:
   Learning to be motivating,
      Expanding Skills for New Horizons!

Engaging in Dramas:
   Casting, Rehearsing, Performing,
      Acting, Role-Playing, Supporting, Bowing!

Cultivating Faith by:
   Studying the Bible, Praying,
      Going out, Serving and Sharing!

NEW DIVERGENCIES:

Growing by Venturing Outwardly:
  Family Relating, Parenting, Mentoring,
    Grandparenting, Supporting and Encouraging.

Learning Culinary Preparations:
  Buying Ingredients, Cleaning them Up!
    Cooking, Seasoning, Serving and Eating Healthy!

Innovating by Writing Poetry:
  Fermenting Ideas for Images,
    Putting Concepts into Words on Paper.

Creative Problem-Solving:
  Defining Problems, Generating Solutions,
    Communicating, making Plan, Evaluating Results!

Sharpening and Shaping Up:
  Engaging in Athletics for Training,
    Conditioning, Exercising, Horse Shoe Pitching.

Multi-Disciplinary Combining:
  Diversifying, Building Up Faith Foundations,
    Seeking Resources Spiritually, Personally, Socially!

Re-developing by Valuing Values:
  Ethical Practicing plus Morally Living,
    Responsible Sexuality; Engaging in Duties!

Personal Self-Developing:
  Physically, Socially, Psychologically,
    Caring for Our Body, Mind, Soul and Spirit!

Reaching out into Communities:
  Involvements in Career Developments,
    Searching, Sustaining and Supporting Others!

Living Fully and Maturely:
Cultivating Gifts, Giving and Receiving,
Committing, Persisting with Determination!

GARDENING LESSONS:

Preparing Soils, Planning, Planting,
Timely Watering, Fertilizing Naturally,
Waiting Patiently, Harvesting, Banquet Celebrating!

Recycling for New Season:
Spreading the Good News, Going Out,
Feeding the Thousands, Working with Nature!

Expressing Gratitude:
Giving Thanks, Reaching Other,
Developing Personally, Socially and Globally.

Teaching Others for growing,
Engaging in Partnerships, Learning,
Working to Improve Quality Living Together!

CONSCIOUSNESS AND AWARENESS

Cultivating consciousness and Awareness
These concepts are also somewhat mysterious!
Fathoming connections from our unconsciousness!

Three facets of each are so very essential!
Investigating these may add to our potential!
This effort builds upon the known for the eventual!

Freud popularized the unconscious!
Jung contributed the collective unconscious!
Both suggested these states are extensive and precious!

The unconscious is largely unknown!
A theoretical concept that cannot be shown!
Scientifically and philosophically, it is postulated!

Two facets are the collective and personal:
The collective is considered as vast and invisible!
Influencing the thoughts and behaviors as plausible!

This great reservoir affects humanity!
Trying to penetrate consciousness eventually!
The ingredients are expressed with personal integrity!

The "pre-conscious" is like a filter!
Screening whether to permit more to emerge!
This may not be considered to a person permissible!

From unconscious through pre-conscious;
What does emerge is lodged in consciousness!
This brain state facilitates neurological processes!

Conscious persons are inward and outward!
Our insights facilitate inner mental development;
Interactions are expressed in a person's environment!

Then there are levels of consciousness!
Altered states occur from brain activities,
Dreams are typical manifestation to is personally!

Other alterations are operational,
Drugs can induce altered states artificially!
Anesthesia also permits surgery rather than painfully!

Psychopathology alters consciousness,
  Schizophrenia and paranoia may be involved!
    Delusions and hallucinations are from altered states!

AWARENESS

Consciousness and awareness are related;
  Awareness typically involved attentiveness!
    Both rational and emotional conditions are perceived!

Both exist within animals with brains.
  Brains facilitate processes for intelligence!
    Cognitive and affective states are both experienced!

Brainwaves measure consciousness!
  If the brain is dead, there is no consciousness!
    The body can function as an organism artificially.

If a person dies with functional organs,
  With permissions they can be transplanted!
    The family can authorize these surgical procedures!

Pain is not felt without consciousness!
  The brain is the seat of conscious processes!
    There are not indications of personal awareness!

Awareness and consciousness are related!
  Awareness does not exist without consciousness!
    And reality is perceived differently in most cultures!

A person may be conscious but not aware!
  Patients loosing awareness may be conscious!
    Often one may assume that they hear but not respond!

Persons may not be aware socially!
    What occurs in their mind is uncertainty!
        Attendants may notice movement but not awareness.

These altered states are known differently!
    Various cultures may use terms known uniquely!
        Because communication is understood with variety.

"Phantasia catalyptica" by the Stoics!
    A phenomenologist describes intentionality!
        Modern German philosophers call it "<u>anwesenheit!</u>"

Professionals and families are advised:
    Assume the person can hear but not respond!
        Conversation is one-way but may be appropriate!

Persons in altered states of consciousness
    They may have degrees of personal awareness!
        Compassionate assumptions may become the wisest!

Persons may emerge from unconsciousness!
    They often have vivid description of experiences!
        If under anesthesia, they are expected to awaken!

Others may have "Near Death Experiences!"
    These are unique and also share similarities!
        Accounts are being captured by research studies.

RESEARCH CAN FACILITATE

Research from a variety of disciplines,
    Are contributing to more understanding!
        These are essential for advancing contributions!

Neurosciences are naturally involved!
   With technology detecting brain activities!
      The brain is a very complex living universe!

Included are human and animal studies!
   There are parallels to fathom complexities!
      Such research is guided by ethical principles!

Measures available now include:
   EEG(Electro Encephalogram) for waves!
      Plus the fMRI(functional magnetic resonance.)

PET(Positron Emission Tomography)
   Plus observable data reported consciously!
SPECT(Single Photon Emission Compute Technology)

Each instrument makes contributions!
   Along with highly technical interpretations!
      Advances are occurring with successive generations!

Theology is beginning to contribute!
   Including our spiritual states of awareness!
      Collaboration is essential for these advancements!

Meditation is another typical variable,
   Plus prayers in diverse forms to be considered!
      Relaxation, yoga, physical exercise plus practices!

Various religions have their own rituals!
   Well-being and health are research variables!
      Included are both objective and subjective measures!

Biology is naturally essential,
   Bodily functions are also very vital!
      Both physiology and spirituality show potential!

Professional cooperation is involved!
Mutual concerns are often readily discovered!
Current and future research will be essential needed!

Many traditional divisions are melting,
Scientists, philosophers and theologians are starting!
Humanity benefits as these collaboration continuing!

IMPRISONMENT<>LIBERATION

Why Are People Imprisoned?

Most persons have awareness of what prisons are since childhood,
Second-hand impressions are known, but others firsthand experience!
Obvious descriptions of prisons include locked gates and window bars,
Plus strange impressions of other prisoners and also armed guards.

Confinement obviously has restrictions of movement typically imposed,
Both physically and mentally an inmate one would be tightly closed.
Prized freedoms are unavailable like one has in the outside world,
The only realm of freedom may be prisoner's creative imagination.

Metaphorically, a prison can be physically, emotionally or personally,
Imprisonment typically is imposed externally, but it can also be denial.
Do you know times when you restricted yourself to a narrow realm?
Have you known of others whose "live lives" within a closed prison?

There are actually "prisoners" who subsist in self-confined narrowness!
It may develop from controlling relationships or sense of helplessness.
Relationships are often stifling particularly within marriage and family,
One member almost becomes a pawn under the finger of relatives.

Combinations of self-to-others are imposed with feelings of entrapment,
No lock-and-key is present, but the mind has such a prisoner's limits.
External controls may be obvious to observers with additional restraints,
The "confined personality" may hardly recognize these arrangements.

Minds and emotions that are locked without typical civil freedoms!
This slave of others may subtly accommodate themselves to another!
A light remark was provided when asked: "How do like marriage?"
He then answered: "It's not bad if you like living in an institution!"

Now after nearly six decades of professional life with observations:
That occasionally a person lives in "jail-like self-imposed prisons!"
From the perspectives of knowing clients, parishioners and students,
Including over 12,000 persons who are known in my professions.

By helping to liberate enclosed minds and bodies then exemplifies,
How entrapment transforms from imprisonment to free personalities!
Psychological problems may place a shell around disturbed patients,
Plus social, financial and structured confinement that are like traps!

Paranoid Schizophrenics are vivid examples of living inside a trap,
So that other people may be actually considered part of a plot.
Sometimes passive persons are the victims of others' aggression,
While obediently complying with external authorities with a passion.

However, internal bars and peculiar world-views may be self-imposed,
There may be little physical evidence of any restraints that are used.
The persons trapped into their own mental processes have symptoms,
Penetrating into this invisible shield that is their self-protections.

Mental patients may be typically locked in treatment-living quarters,
But the visible limits on movement are secondary to their minds.
The metaphors of imprisonment and entrapment may be fitting,
Inside their thinking are few open windows or doors opening.

A caution is timely because self-imprisonment is different from jails,
But a person's own restricting guards can be internalized walls.
This sense of being snared into "strangeness and peculiar-ness,"
Become distinctive characteristics of self-imposed imprisonments.

It may be difficult to imagine the internal functioning of clients,
Even expert professionals are unable to "get inside" these patients.

The may be layers of bars and thick walls of protective shells.
　　The exaggerated claims in inappropriate that they live in hells!

Functioning freely has subjective parameters known only inside,
　　Even minor degrees of liberation can be exciting or threatening.
Persons protect themselves from wide arrays of their environments,
　　In order to preserve their self-image from injurious experiences.

LIBERATING CASE STUDIES

Recently published biographical accounts involve the Russian prisons:
　　Just Send Me Word: A True Story of Love and Survival in the Gulag![38]
Lev Mishchenko and Svetlana Ivanova exchanged over 1200 letters,
　　The author, Orlando Figes, provides details of miraculous survival!

The review of this book is written by Michael Scammell's account,
　　Entitled "Love Against All Odds," published in the New York Review.
The inspirations from this book and review are incorporated now,
　　As illustrative case studies of how persons have learned to grow.

As university physics students, Lev and Sventlana became acquainted,
　　But as World War II progressed, so did Stalin's vast imprisonments.
For over a decade, they articulated their experiences in their letters,
　　Their intense dedication helped them survive to unite in their marriage.

This biography describes their deliberate refusals to give up hope,
　　Apparently, these fragile communications inspired both to then cope.
Physical hardship and vicious inmates overcome by humanizing prison,
　　They focused on their assignments to make "the best of the worst!"

Without these biographical accounts, we would not gain their insights,
　　Like a few other survivors in the gulags and in the holocaust trials,
They both found strength to discover personal meaning for each other,
　　Rather than giving up into a shell, their remembrances were vital.

---

[38]　Figes, O., 2012, Just Send Me Words: A True Story of Love & Survival in the Gulag, Metropolitan Press.

One external observation is that meaning is found with other persons,
    When someone is significant to another, extraordinary fortitude exists.
Here is my personal affirmation: "I find meaning when I an important
    To someone who is important to me!" derived from Victor Frankl!

Frankl survived Auschwitz during this same period of World War II,
    He kept focused on his purpose in of his life plus also his relatives.
These accounts are contrasts with the self-encased entrapments
    About circumstances of inhumane treatments during imprisonments.

These positive cases vividly contrast with self-imposed confinements,
    Suggesting the essential benefit of personal goals and relationships.
Reaching out to an entrapped mental patient may be their lifeline,
    Revealing the special significance that is part of real exchange.

Friendships are likewise exceedingly important in social interactions,
    Personal connections can be more vital than professional relations.
Collaborating with each other is a facet of "Eusociality" conceptually,
    The new exciting current book: The Social Conquest of the Earth![39]

"Eusociality" is the key dynamic of cooperation for species to survive,
    Wilson gleans his half-century of scientific research how we are alive.
He pioneered the discipline encased in "Socio-Biology" with optimism,
    Discovered from numerous vertebrates and invertebrates their socialism.

This model incorporates Politics, Economics, Biology and Psychology,
    Plus his affinity for appreciating Religion, Education and Sociology.
His in-depth research about the origins of species over millenniums,
    Discovers how surviving species foster their collaborative cooperation.

His discoveries challenge a century old concept of limited altruism.
    This theory suggests that species only sacrifice for genetic relatives.
While selfish motives have prevailed by using violence and war,
    These destructive attacks could annihilate much of living creatures.

Wilson's rationale is based on comprehensive altruism for community,
    That colonies for self-perpetuating generations are found in their unity.

---

[39]   Wilson, E.O., 2012, The Social Conquest of the Earth!,

As species we have learned socially and biologically to foster survival,
   Have the edge in lasting in hostile environments to become livable.

These concepts challenge the propensity to advance more competition,
   Selfish motivations he finds are destructive for succeeding generations.
His hopeful optimism provides strategies to foster living cooperation,
   So that creation has hopeful futures by refining their collaboration.

12. ADAPTABILITY

Liberating Strategies

Several fields have launched into liberating methods for future hope,
   Reaching back to how ocean creatures evolved into land species.
Otherwise, living only in water was confinement to this container,
   While evolution over millions and billions of years is the refiner.

Schools of certain aquatic species thrived by living in schools,
   Massive numbers of fish genetically swim by large numbers,
This general model is illustrative of land liberation from water,
   Upon the Earth's surface, these communities joined even later.

In contemporary imaginations are seeds of living in outer space,
   Astronauts demonstrate explore possibilities for the human race.
Birds have mastered both flight and surface existence for example,
   Our creative imagination and technological discoveries as models.

Liberation Theology is another strategy for escaping from poverty,
   The plight of the poor becomes the focus of Biblical teachings.
Power structures have tried to squelch practices of honoring poor,
   By Economic disparities where the rich exploit with their control.

Free market competition functions for the powerful with resources,
   Crassly, the wealthy control this imprisonment of those poorer.

Class conflicts are the insipient dynamics for rebels to revolt,
To overpower their dominators with more equal treatment!

The struggles of poorer castes[40] to be liberated from enslavement,
Often becomes violent war that consumes enormous human costs.
If the human and subhuman species survive only as the fittest,
Fighting each other to extinction is disastrous destiny in futures.

Liberation strategies are also entering political strategies on earth,
Cooperative efforts are essential for sustainable living in futures.
The social ethics and preservation of the environment is at stake,
Sustainable strategies become a primary criterion to be engaged.

In imprisonment, captives are prone to use methods for survival,
One is "Identification with the Aggressor" to obtain positive favors.

Prisoners may identify with the power of guards to do punishment,
So that becoming like the aggressor is considered appropriate.

This is similar to the assumption that we imitate the wealthy,
That everyone wants the rich to live like the rich to be selfish.
While these rationalizations may politically gain voter emulation,
There is destructive strategy for more unsustainable consumption

Liberation psychology ideally aims to free people from themselves,
Fostering self-giving actions so that everyone eventually benefits.
These ideals are readily short-circuited as liberators imitate power,
Identifying with the powerful rather than liberating the prisoner.

The higher ideals of advancing the common good to recover,
Yes, this strategy is vulnerable to threatening "power-players!"
Liberating implementers who hold to species survival are learning,
This optimizes the energetic efforts of more creativity for thriving.

---

[40]   Wilkerson, I.S., 2020 CASTES: The Origins of our Discontents, Random
House, Yew York.

Political strategies that advance the well-being of their citizenry,
Inherently are liberating the imprisoned without fairer equality.
The old top-down hierarchy of the "pecking orders" is outdated,
Collaborative efforts conjoin cooperators to become liberators.

Natural genetics combined with "Eusociality"[41] has provocative ideas,
Humanity can foster liberation of the cooperative living creatures!
Destructive violence may be overcome in time with peaceful justice,
So that both the earth and living species may become liberated!

Yes, these concepts are positive ideals that will also be criticized,
Motivated more by hopeful optimism than pessimistically resigned!
Destiny involves returned to earthly dust only after contributing,
Toward deliberate liberation over resignation to more imprisoning.

Human ingenuity is essential as neurosciences advance brains,
Divine destinies stretch humanity to reach beyond past restraints.
Conjoined together, creative forces move toward more liberation,
So that small measurable steps are taken by each generation!

GLOBALIZATION

From the old parochial to new global,
This is a long stretch in the overall!
A human often thinks she/he is center
Assuming the world focuses on their banter!

Cultures and nations are also self-centered!
Along with their practices that are exercised!
Old boundaries are like wall around boxes,
Countries consider impositions as losses!

---

[41]   *Op.cit.* Wilson, E.O.,

One's own language narrows one's viewpoints
As well as their religion, foods and relations!
Leaders typically are known to be very tribal!
Making their chosen enemies their own rivals!

New ideas are often considered with suspicion!
Strangers are to be dangerously malicious!
When struggles attempt to take away power
Control is contentious testing for cowards!

SCHOOLING AND EDUCATION

Prior to Education, Schooling had dominated!
Informal training is then culturally inculcated!
Geography is narrowed down to what is local!
Outside the tribe is usually seen as foreign!

Just one language is also solely learned!
Rare individuals have two communicated!
Occasionally, inter-marriages have occurred
Prompting careful interactions to be learned!

Geo-political exchanges are very carefully made!
Cautious maneuvers are involved and foreign aid!
Ignorance and fearfulness feed uneasy tensions!
And testy actions are done with apprehension!

Cultural religions are often very mysterious!
Rituals and Divinities cause suspiciousness.
But trusting relationships can be cultivated
By inquisitiveness that may become suspected!

Educational exchanges open our minds!
Both Youth and Adults get new finds!
Jewish, Muslim, Hindu and Buddhism
Geo-religions providing us with wisdom!

Study abroad and hosting new visitors
Enlarge our minds to be appreciators!
Personally knowing about these cultures,
Creates for us, new interpersonal friends!

LANGUAGES

Cultural people appreciate our efforts
To learn about their own basic terms!
Geo-languages expand our verbiage
As we try to speak other languages!

India has at least 100 basic languages![42]
But Hindi, Urdu and English enlarge!
They often speak English very rapidly
Typical for people exchanging culturally!

Many Westerners use French, German or English;
Now Spanish and Chinese give further reach!
Human languages are learned very quickly
Children in communicate languages early!

Global Internets encourage new varieties!
These tele-devices are in numerous cultures
These exchanges facilitate on-line education,
Plus reaching far into international relations!

---

[42] Three invitations to India have informed the author.

GEO-METRICS, -ECONOMICS, -JUSTICE

Temperatures include degrees and centimeters!
Adapting quickly is essential for new travelers!
Inches, feet and yards convert to geometrics!
Global accommodations are not just gimmicks!

Trade is facilitated by converting measures!
Each culture values its own dear treasurers!
Markets expand globally to other countries!
Attracting producer and consumer exchanges!

Cosmologists hold that life emerged from minute' particles,
Thereafter over billions of years, life became very diverse.
Only in recent eras did reflective consciousness occur,
Emerging in brains of human beings and few animals.

Consciousness contrasts with pre-conscious and unconscious.
Distinctions help with comprehension of awareness mysteries.
Do primitive creatures possess awareness of themselves?
In propagation, males and females recognize their species.

Self-consciousness by non-humans is difficult to detect,
One method is having an animal look into a mirror to reflect.
Primitive species do not notice any of their self-awareness,
Just chimpanzees indicate they discover self-consciousness!

Human infants slowly realize their distinctions from Mother.
This self-awareness is a step toward being another person.
Individual personhood is debated and very controversial,
Fertilized embryos do not possess what to them is personal.

Neurosciences emerge in contemporary research studies,
Consciousness is among the subjects of more new theories.

Brain MRI provides more images of blood flowing actively,
   Inferring that brain functioning is more concentrated locally.

Research about altered consciousness has many reports,
   Sleep is one of the common states that animals do regularly.
REM sleep signals a dream is occurring to protect sleep,
   This refers to "Rapid Eye Movement" when sleep is deep.

Pre-consciousness is illustrated by "tip-of-the-tongue!"
   By realizing we know something but cannot recall that instant.
Anticipation of an event about to occur is pre-conscious,
   Basic brain functioning comes before our fuller awareness.

In mid-19th century, anesthesia was medically discovered,
   Ether soon became surgeons altered state to be preferred.
Other chemical compounds can also induce unconsciousness.
   So that patients do not experience pain in their awareness.

In past decades, a few surgical patients experience pain,
   But most cannot move or talk to report what has begun.
A few even are haunted by this pain that did take place,
   Influencing their sensitivities to an unconscious state.

Surgeons and executioners have been very concerned,
   One instrument that registered unconsciousness was used.
This spectrometer(BIS) that detects electrical activity,
   Within a range band, patients do not realize consciously.

However, recent research discovered the BIS is inaccurate,
   Quickly prompting surgeons to create another technique.
Dr. Guilo Tomoni[43] developed the "qauliascope" visually,
   This is replacing the inadequate BIS now used in surgery.

---

[43]   Long, Joshua, Jan-Feb. 2013 "Awakening" in The Atlantic.

Tomoni designates "phi" as his symbol to consciousness,
In his galaxy images he states: "Within this dusty universe,
Would be stars that would be every living consciousness!"
"Consciousness Theory" he researches at U. of Wisconsin.

Related research fields involve "After Death Experiences,"
They have conscious awareness returning to consciousness.
One Neurosurgeon[44] has written about his own awareness,
Claiming his unconscious state has distinct differences.

These experiences after death as declared can be ominous,
Prompting people to register altered state of being conscious.

With neurosciences discovering more and more intricacies,
Stimulates more respect for the human brain's magnificence!

At this stage of study, the brain has 85-100 billion neurons,
Multi-thousands of connections into greater complexities.
Estimates are around seven trillion intricate connections,
This "universe" is between our ears for brain locations.

Both neurosciences and cosmological physics is expansive,
Particularly realizing the universe out there is expanding.
There is such a vast aspects of creation is not understood,
Mysteries and uncertainties depict awareness as it unfolds.

---

[44] 2013 article in my library of references.

IV. FUTURISTICALLY

GLOPEACE

Our globe yearns for peace and justice!
And global conflicts have been on ISIS!
Violence persists & becomes senseless!
Producing weapons for sale is reckless!

Being constructive leads to production!
By countering downfalls of destruction!
Major contributions are very creative!
Building societies is extremely positive!

Humanity inter-connects by technology!
Bringing people in contact instantly!
Our national boundaries are obsolete!
Increasingly people are interdependent!

River, oceans and mountains are "trans-versed;"
Likewise boundaries are so rapidly dispersed!
Space transmitters convey quad-trillions
To 7.3+ billions in global population!

Oil transport for power adds to global warming!
The results of CO_2 are rapidly accumulating!
Food products are increasingly required!
Water is needed to grow and be harvested!

Solar and wind energy is really needed!
Balancing fossil fuels from coal and oil!
Conservative imagination and technology
Provides for nine billion+ people by 2050!

EVOLUTIONARY SCIENCES
AND SPIRITUALITY

Many disciplines incorporate concepts of evolution for explanations,
Just a few illustrations are mentioned to catch readers' attention.
Assuming there is an educated knowledge of Darwin's concepts,
These social sciences already have incorporates his theories.

In Psychology, there are influences that readily become apparent,
The highly endowed person will generally be most competent.
Numerous factors influence human development about growth,
Obviously genetics and environment reflect nature and nurture.

Biochemistry enlightens humanity about the survival of the fittest,
Sociology and Anthropology provide evidence now and the past.
Interaction of these fields results in providing Social Anthropology,
Combining human and animal behaviors emerged as Sociobiology.

E.O. Wilson at Harvard helps the delivery of these two twins,
His new book also promises to provide new research finding.
He is concerned with evidence of insect's group collaboration,
He synthesizes evolutionary and socio-behavior in cooperation.

Evolutionary and also Behavioral Economics stimulate each other,
Exploring rational and emotional decision-making in the markets.
Understanding insight from Theology and History makes contributions,
These individual disciplines benefit from exploratory combinations.

Evolutionary Economics is explored by Frank at Cornell University,
He evaluates both the free markets and the planned economies.
Recognizing the dated aphorism by a Founder of Free Enterprise,
Evaluating A. Smith's assumption about "The Invisible Hand of God."[45]

---

[45]   Smith, Adam

There are often polarizations touted by proponents of a discipline,
  So that the extreme explanations are advocated by dominance.
Ideologies that are tested with empirical research also do benefit,
  Discovering that polar opposites both contain truthful evidence.

In all of these Sciences whether Natural, Math or Social fields,
  Initially discover tensions that immaturely may be separated.
With research and dialogues, fields begin to discover compatibility,
  As paradoxical thinking helps resolve tensions thru discoveries.

Theology also benefits from comprehending broad human nature,
  Are human beings primarily good or are real people actually evil?
Philosophical experiences assist in resolving these real tensions,
  Including a number of paradoxes that provide tense harmonies.

Further examples informed by both Science and Faith are available,
  Science advocates inductive reasoning, Religion is more deductive.
Both search for truth for the benefit of humanity in real societies,
  Efforts to blend their insights have contributions with harmony.

There are understandable experiences of conflicts in reconciliation,
  Extreme thinking may often bi-furcate humanity by polarization.
These conflicts can be addressed for the eventual benefit of all,
  With awareness that conflicts stimulate creativity and resolve.

While extremes in human and natural conflicts may be stressful,
  Research in creative thinking provides evidence that is insightful.
"Creativity is constructive response to stress" from Paul Torrance,
  Can be empirically researched to reveal both growth and success.

Here are a series of questions that could be examined beneficially:

- How can evolution be incorporated to explain free-market Economics?
- Are market decisions made rationally to maximum profitability?

- *Theologically, how does the "Hand of God" operate in any economy?*

In human development, additional hypotheses are due examination:

- *What are optimal interactions of Genetics and environment in growth?*
- *Can cognitive, social, emotional and artificial intelligence influence creativity?*
- *What is the relation among Neuroscience and Cultural Anthropology?*

When considering the relationships among Faith and Empirical Science:

- *How does intercessory prayer influence a patient's recovery?*
- *In what dimensions does faith development influence morality?*
- *What are inferences from uncertainties of quantum mechanics?*
- *What are worthwhile hypotheses to investigated Faith and Science?*

Here are issues for understanding Creation and Cosmology:

- *How do creation myths correspond to expanding multi-verses?*
- *Where are the compatibility plus irreconcilable differences?*
- *Is the earth the primary site for Divine-Human encounters?*

When disciplines discover tensions, each can become stimulated,
To make efforts in bridge-building rather than further polarized.
These strategies become synergistic to formulate testable hypotheses.
Both polar opposites are provocative in advancing Faith and Science!

ORIENTATION TO EMERGING PROBLEMS

Now campaigns are going, many winners and losers are making reflections,
This is time for re-grouping, rethinking, and analyzing these recent elections.

There are more than political parties that now operate openly in this game,
There are also wild cards that privately wield influence in order to find fame.

The Supreme Court's ruling in February, 2010, opened up corporate funding,
The influence of money is shifting from usual rules to more free marketing.

It is not surprising that wealthy sources consider the government up for sale,
Wealthy interests in Corporate Boards are now beyond the traditional pale.

It is not new that democracy would again be threatened by return to oligarchy,
Wealthy people in back rooms have frequently tried to kidnap democracy.

Governments have often wrestled with the influence of very special interest,
Control concentrated by a powerful few can override the best for the rest.

An assumption prevails that the self-interested do not need external regulation,
With foxes guarding the henhouse, accountable oversight yields to collusion.

Regulated industries and financial institutions plant their own in Congress,
Pretense of monitoring violations of laws and regulations is even worse.

Governments at all levels are susceptible to domination by actual violators,
Independent judgment has been jeopardized by such flagrant manipulators.

When expectations of people are climbing but in decline in the world of reality
Researchers and Theoreticians have models foreseeing revolution potentiality.

The future in many global crises are easily ignored or diverted from locally,
Denial and diversion are old games that can distract an uninformed citizenry.

Little reading is required to understand history or to notice changes globally,
Many corporations have more global control than nations have politically.

Democracies are very vulnerable to manipulation for the control by a few,
Masses of the other citizens are then wondering what exactly they can do?

The roles of political parties are no longer the organized groups in control,
Media owned by slanted private interests, do you believe what you're told?

MORE APPARENT SYMPTOMS OF ILLNESS

The American colonies were once under the rule of the British government,
After 150 years of being 13 colonies, revolution occurred in a brief moment.

Analogously the powerful United States currently treats countries as colonies,
We are facing resistance and rebellion of rising powers who hate tyrannies.

Very few of current American leaders are well-aware of these rapid changes,
Many live in a shell of protection without comprehending modern array.

Arrogant leaders have sounded disrespectful, condescending and superior,
A large number of them sound like adolescents who are in need to mature.

It is easy for inflated egos to over-estimate what is really their significance,
There are mounds of data to doubt their haughty claims as more evidence.

The proof of their self-centeredness is their pride in their own leadership.
Lack of collaboration reveals their incapacities to engage in partnerships.

Quickly over-stepping their limited roles in legislation they sound inflated,
Their self-centeredness presumes that they speak for all citizens are dated.

Their quick self-elevation is a symptom of their nauseous individualism.
This over-stated influence feeds their pre-occupation with socialism.

This country is more vulnerable because leaders are noticeably unaware,
Without realizing that rising global powers notice our inability to share.

Government leaders understandably find this special interest bewildering,
Wealthy manipulators can be out of visual sight but even more controlling.

What can be done when the Judges on the Supreme Court become activists?
Just Faith in the three Branches of Government may not be able to exist?

HIDDEN SYPMPTOMS
BELOW THE SURFACE!

Perceptive analysts can understand from outside observation from a distance,
America is very Xenophobic so that the populist is dominated by resistance.

The rising democracies in the world are subject to very similar manipulation,
Moneyed interests can concentrate wealth that is managed by a corporation.

Just a few thinkers realize that chartering a corporation has obvious danger,
Created by the state, corporation charters are fueled now by incendiary anger.

America and the free world needs to have much better global understandings,
The future of humanity could depend upon much greater depth in findings.

Political parties and candidates are readily influenced by very clever tactics,
The whole realm of government is gradually changing to go beyond politics.

Religious views easily are deceived by separating from government and politics,
With these incremental models we need to have more than one-sided clerics.

This mess may be frustrating because it provides few clear and definite answers,
However, constructive questions are important to envision the new futurists.

Now crucial pending disasters are not currently apparent are being ignored,
These are confirmed scientific research findings that are simply postponed.

Future generations who will suffer from this neglect are not being considered,
The immediate agendas of short-sighted officials are instead being pushed.

These symptoms accumulate so gradually that their effects are not noticed,
So the long-range health of the young is being deferred and not prevented.

If a frog is placed into water at low temperature and increasingly heat it.
Frogs do not leap out as slow gradual temperature rises boiling to die hot.

Obvious needs are bridges between scientific researchers and policy-makers.
There are many selfish interests in profits that do not make wise investors.

When our decision-makers are unable or unwilling to face potential disasters,
Future generation will surely suffer from these notably stubborn deciders.

The problems with immediate gain results from short-range selfish thinking,
The next election or next balance sheets are symptoms now are coming.

Dangerously ominous but far-off damaging storms receive little attention;
Fear that is considered imminent, stamps out concerns of future generations.

Short-range issues can ignite fears that are used as threats for motivations,
These are conjured up so that voters are duped into more narrow decisions.

There already is gross neglect in protection of clean air and pure water,
These are vital for Creation for whom humans are expected to be protector.

Our atmosphere and natural resources are treasures that are very fragile,
Responsible stewardship demands sacrifice now rather than being casual.

When politicians have their pet agenda they do not hesitate to invoke God,
God is co-opted as a tool to threaten voters who are not perceptive of fraud.

Conservatives politically contradict commitment in their conversation,
Consumption now is openly marketed rather than resource preservation.

Contradictory agendas are as ancient as the highest geologically old hills,
The analytical skills of today's voters actually have very few tested skills.

Another pattern involves people of like minds talking in chambers that echo.
They talk to themselves enclosed in stovepipes! compartments! or a silo!

There are few windows in these echo chambers as they listen to themselves,
Lyrics are more like self-talk without listening to contrary views like elves.

Insulated from challenges, they hype-up their narrow outlook of worldviews,
Without hearing other perspectives, they reinforce their clubs with high dues.

13. SURFACE POLITICAL DIAGNOSTICS

Many rigid officials are stuck in the past of their own inertia with designs,
    They fight dirty and hard to retain their own power to staying in trenches.

A new generation will wipe them out in the developing future in due time,
    Change is rapidly occurring so that old leadership will be in the decline.

On-line services are already in rapid communication that is global in scope,
    Anyone unacquainted and also resistant will soon be considered a dope!

Old line politicians are a very threatened species so they will fight vigorously,
    They want to keep power and control so they will likely make great miseries.

The rising global world powers may soon quickly pass by the United States,
    Without adjusting to these realities Americans will be left in their wakes.

Many Americans are suffering from dangerously coronavirus diseases?
    People fear innumerable diseases that threaten our health and well-being.

Imaginary and actual dangers stymie us so we readily take new precautions.
    Not only reality and professional diagnosis balances our vivid imaginations.

AIDS in the past decades many vulnerable people were extremely frightened,
    A long process of deterioration and decline may be mysterious and lingered.

We become concerned about possible illnesses that may occur in an infant,
    The threats of incurable, impairing maladies receive concerns in an instant.

Increasingly we now know more about both physical and mental incapacity,
    We do not want to be handicapped or decimated as we move with tenacity,

Now our concerns about our brains and bodies cannot be easily over-stated,
    Insurance, hospitals, specialists, therapy and pharmaceuticals aren't abated.

Shifting from fear of personal illness concerns are extended to the body Politics,
    We're comfortable with describing the free market as impaired in Economics.

It is frightening that our political governance is infected inside and internal,
Some of these illnesses are treatable while other cancers become terminal.

In a diagnostic metaphor, might our body politic have undetected distress?
It is not readily detected with any type of Cat-Scan, X-Ray or blood tests.

A 30-year Congressman unbelievably shelters ignorance about taxes,
Recently he told a public audience that there are 45% who pay no taxes!

He pandered to his audience with pleasant word many liked to hear him say,
Overlooking over 20% of sales taxes, property and employment they pay.

He ignored numerous gas and sales taxes are high to support governments,
But he submitted his views as if they were very informed true statements.

We have numerous officials who are involved in issues that are misleading,
They raise the issues like homosexuality, abortion, and too much taxing.

They are beholden to vested interests from big corporations and Wall Street,
Insurance, Big Oil, and Auto Industry are also to whores who are lobbyists.

Many middle management are organizationally intimidated by their votes,
Even when their bosses subtly pressure them more to get into their boats.

These officials deny neglect of children, pure air and water for protection,
They readily rely upon manufactured fears plus God and slanted religions.

They are ambivalent about understanding the problems of our environment,
They tend to assume that their seat in government should be permanent.

Their focus on the future is very selectively tentative and full of speculation,
Rarely do some ever show concern about the health of God's own Creation.

Sam Khater, an economist writes: "The Rich are Different; they are Ruthless!"
They don't hesitate taking advantage of poorly impoverished who are helpless.

"The wealthy deny irresponsibility about home loans and foreclosures!"
Defaulters are thrashed and other properties in the area decline in values!

Financiers do not seem to have the civic ethic and morals helping and friendly.
Rich investors may have less responsibility both financially or neighborly.

Do we want a political party that attracts wealthy who foreclose on mortgages?
Who are tending to be selfish neighbors in depressed economic hard times?

Lord Acton[46] observed the excesses and temptations of political power clearly:
His brilliant aphorism: "Power corrupts; absolute power corrupts absolutely!"

Public Officials with inflated egos may not know their leadership is pompous,
In managing personal and organizational power many wielded too vicious.

Humility is a very scarce quality for leaders who practice control politically,
Human beings considered too selfish as expressed immoral and unethically!

Now it is very appropriate to learn how to develop relations respectively;
Humanity benefits from better understanding on how to relate morally.

Reinhold Niebhur[47] wrote during the Great Deep Depression and World War II:
"Democracy is possible because of the goodness in man;
Democracy is necessary because of the evil in man!"
SO VOTE for the BEST CANDIDATE not JUST THEIR POLITCIAL PARTY,
DETECT IF THEY'RE NEIGHBORS WHO ARE TRULY TRUSTWORTHY!

DEEP POLITICAL DIAGNOSTICS

Going underneath the surface of shallow media and superficial candidates,
Could fevers and symptoms be invisible to us viewers in campaign debates?

Could there be impairing deterioration very deep inside the political body?
Using a clinical model, let's explore what is now undetectable to anybody.

Polarities in political parties has gone beyond the pale of the ethical rules,
Influence is concentrated in wealthy people who fund many hidden pools.

---

[46]   Acton, Lord
[47]   Niebuhr, Reinhold

Courts can comprehend laws but overlook "WE THE PEOPLE!" unconsciously!
If Federal Judges are out of touch, how might we have greater accountability?

Appointed justices have been known to serve on the bench but not fully alive,
Even Bishops are required to retire when they reach the age of seventy-five.

One solution is term limits so that justices are appointed for a specified time,
Otherwise senility, Alzheimer, Dementia and physical limits begin to decline.

Many cultures have dominated many cultures by authoritarian patriarchy,
Courageous minorities and women have challenged traditions appropriately.

Our current practices in government have numerous perceptive critics,
Is it not essential that transformation happens in the practice of politics?

Are the three branches of democratic governance becoming more proactive?
We need both concerned citizens and brilliant minds to be more effective.

Who will advocate more for the civil protection of our numerous minorities?
Human beings in "Group Think," easily advance exclusively the majorities.

Democracy demands that all participants act with more social responsibility!
Officials best comprehend that the Divine expects mortals to accountability.

Freedom is not for just a few privileged but genuine freedom is to share,
The essential paradoxes of free civil rights demand intentionality to care.

Government officials are detached when they are guided only by ideologies,
Enlightened discoveries of ethicists are that we are assured full equalities.

Human beings create artificial systems of authority to which they adhere,
Their deductive logic needs constant testing beyond inciting primarily fear.

History is replete with powerful persons who are really out of close touch,
Ivy Halls, stovepipe silos and specialization may have become too much!

Rebalance is necessary plus envisioning the vision of humanity's futures,
We cannot live just in the past or the present but tomorrow's new cultures.

Better equilibrium between extreme polarities is needed to find resolution,
Extremists rarely advocate moderation in any of their one-sided solutions.

14. WHAT ARE POSSIBLE TREATMENTS?

The French press was the Fourth Estate that reported honesty in government,
The three branches of democracy were suspect to be some degree redundant.

Media today are a megaphone with limited concern for integrity and accuracy,
Current media are dominated by violence and persons who are largely angry.

The Press is not really free but pressured to produce profits and advertising;
Many respectable newspapers have closed because they are not profiting.

At least there are respectable media guided by responsible journalism ethics,
While uncontrolled IT communication prompts primarily brief sound bites.

Some persons' brains cannot carry on rational discussion or be analytical,
Instant news splatters across the TV screen for attention that is volatile.

TV reporters' beauty deceives viewers as persons without in-depth reports,
Public audiences are impatient because they have more interest in sports.

It is obvious that media are primarily motivated by profitable commercial,
Western Press becomes untrustworthy because they need to be profitable.

It is disturbing about co-opting honorable persons who are professionals,
Their political interests become primarily what will be most profitable.

From direct observational research, this motive influences many managerial,
Also affected is the honesty of people in professions typically known as legal.

Medical and Education professionals have become noticeably entrepreneurial.
Dental, Accounting and clerical professionals have also neglected being critical.

Even the offspring of the state have taken over the wellbeing of their own sire,
Have we arrived at the mixture of economic and political interest as so dire?

Will future generations wonder about the practices of contemporary enterprises,
History might teach lessons of catastrophes that seeded subsequent quagmires.

When the parasites and leeches are so deeply embedded into the body politic,
The progressing cancers slowly take over the entire carrier to become tragic.

Timely analysis needs to penetrate now to the causes and not just the symptoms,
In order for both treatment and prevention to preclude deeply rooted problems.

These causes are very complex so that consultation by many experts is needed,
If their quick advice is too shallow to discover causes they should not be heeded.

These complicated societal dilemmas have become embedded with deep roots,
Quick fixes like band aid cover the symptoms but not recognize their shoots.

It is essential to continuously update efforts to discover penetrating diagnosis,
Then the best available treatment and prevention will have a better prognosis.

DIAGNOSTICS

Do we comprehend human minds?
Each thinking person has this kind!
Individually, a mind is mysterious!
Countering explanations as obvious!

Minds are invisible to other persons!
While minds are needed to do lessons!
Our mind and brain are connected
These "siblings" are closely related!

They are mysteriously able to multiply!
They can disclose what is, and also why!
Helping us to understand and to comply
Sometimes, they are ready to stand by!

Location of our own mind is evasive!
Producing thoughts may be persuasive!
Our brain is essential for us "to know!"
This internal process tells us why and how!

IMAGINATION: WHAT IS HAPPENING?

Humanity fosters our imagination!
Building contemporary civilizations!
All of North and South, East and West
Continue developing the next crest!

Dreaming stirs up our imagination!
Providing risk-takers with motivation!
By striving for changes constructively!
Responding to pressures creatively!

Some organizations face stagnation
Prompting responses with regression!
When struggling to fulfill their mission!
Hoping old practices create additions.

These situations need analytical study,
Diagnosing the causes of such rigidity!
Defining problems that need solving!
Creative approaches can then resolve!

MODERN MENTORING

Mentoring is an important quality!
By assisting to increase credibility!
Young persons are beneficiaries!
Mentors are rewarded intangibly!

New value can become strategies!
For your consideration as qualities!
Add positive! "Encourage Mentors!"
Mentees gain wisdom of benefactors!

Even further: "Beyonder Mentors!"
Help mentees go beyond predictors!
By surprising familiar observers
Assisting those who are similar!

"Encouraging Mentors" are positive!
Countering predictions as negative!
Affirming younger is also supportive
Encourage-Mentors are affirmative!

DISCERNING

Discernment is a key capability!
Discerning truth of possibilities!
By evaluating among alternatives
In decision processes as positive!

"Discern+Mentor=Discern Mentors!"
Personally plus also internationally!
Weighing options as recommended
Valuable in family and community!

Life confronts mentees with decisions!
Deciding choices by evaluations!
All our decisions are significant
Discerners can become important!

FACING FUTURE CONFUSIONS

Contemporary outlook experiences confusion:
The economy, virus and political delusion.
A "Fortress Model" is now descriptive;
Attempting to see what is prescriptive.

The Conservatives look out their fort;
They see many dangers that may erupt!
Everyone outside are seen as dangerous;
Enemies are threatening their fortress!

Moderates look out and have confusion;
They cannot arrive at some resolution.
Who are Friends? Or Enemies out there?
They keep the drawbridges up in despair.

Liberals with a Fort, open the gates!
They open the drawbridge and run out!
They hug everyone outside this new fort;
"We're not threats! We are all friends!"

Now who will catch the coronavirus?
Those without masks who are huggers!
Who will starve without food in the fort?
What will solve problems for the moderates?

The future faces major uncertainties;
How will change be handled by humanity?
Decisions will obviously have challenges;
The unfolding future has many edges!

CREATING!

Balancing conformity and creativity!
Creativeness is a valuable quality!
This step opens "Creative-Mentors!"
Encouragement to become originators!

Envisioning possibilities is essential!
For creators to reach their potential!
Favorable envisioning is supportive!
Helping teams to become collaborative!

Discovering new solutions is needed!
Cultures encourage what is expected!
Mentors typically value imaginations!
So mentors produce original creations!

Good News about coronavirus vaccinations!
Researchers have found a key solution.
Europeans have been the new discoverers;
Humanity will become the benefactors.

RISK-TAKING

New products demand risk-taking!
Encouragement to develop undertakings!
Most risks flourish on leading edges!
Exploring builds new knowledges!

The ability to learn from mistakes,
Because fewer mistakes facilitates!
But making mistakes fast is helpful
Learning what needs correction!

Mentoring also benefits many skills!
Ready to engage in change and schools!
Personal sensitivity of key differences
Raises constructive questions and answers!

When to motivate or to wait!
Productive inquiries for bait!
Learn together by collaboration!
Tailoring key future consultations!

Letting go as the younger proceeds
Consult later as there are needs!
For more independent adventures!
Launching themselves to futures!

15. PROFOUND PARADOX
OF HUMAN EXISTENCE

When contemplating the extensive Universe in which we all live,
Provocative thoughts are stimulated for why we are alive.
Astronomers the past two centuries have expanded our worlds,
As humans are even more insignificant as creation unfurls.

One paradoxical expression may be "significantly Insignificant!"
Our existence is so miniscule that we are known as minute.'
In contrast, as creative beings we are "Infinitely so Indefinite!"
This can also be expressed in the words "Infinitely Finite!"

A paradox describes humans as so "Predictably Unpredictable!"
We have both consistency along with being so unreliable.
We have characterized ourselves as being so physically pliable,
But humans also express terms like "Spiritually Invincible!"

SCIENTIFIC INVESTIGATIONS

As our Universe is explored for dark matter and dark energy,
   We simultaneously benefit and overwhelmed scientifically.
When we have conflicting goals can our perceptions be trusted?
   How essential are the criteria for science to be objective?

Space explorers now suggest we only know about five percent,
   The great unknown obviously to us humans is enormous.
Fortunately, we have come to realize that we are pliably dynamic,
   In contrast to earlier beliefs that humans are rigidly static.

We have the capacities to both be so stuck and also stubborn,
   We can provoke fellow humans into dynamics of reform.
The processes are considered facet of being transformational,
   As a result, we are also involved being repeatedly cyclical.

Spiritual and scientific explorations uncover new developments.
   Will we even consider the two forces as being compliments?
The Universe "out there" can be explored and also be measurable,
   Complimenting these objects, prompts what is treasurable.

Our worlds both externally and internally are now expanding,
   These forces hopefully help us resist opposite contracting.
We often retreat in the face of fears of the unknown and scary,
   Courage is essential for future generations to find bravery.

Foundations of adventure are now being laid into the future,
   The spirit of discovery will help human explore nature.
Geologists, Archeologists, Anthropologists and Cosmologists,
   Are scientifically investigating the far deepest recesses.

We are also investigating ourselves as inherently in nature,
   These are challenges that expect us to be more objective.

Coping with subjectivity may be an impossible expectation,
This forces humans to realize we are part of creation.

Are external observations essential to understand who we are?
Can we accurately examine ourselves while we also care?
This prompts human Scientists to confront their limitation,
Objectivity is impossible when we are in transformation.

Unanswered issues require even more profound exploration,
How can the paradox be resolved into accurate formation?
While there has been intriguing discoveries of what is out there,
Are we ready to investigate what is deeply inside us here?

TENTATIVE OBSERVATIONS

The epistemological issues are profound and also disturbing,
How can human creatures still claim to know everything?
If Scientists' assumptions hold that only observable is real,
Does this claim presume that humans are vastly surreal?

Less we become inflated with our limited human perceptions,
Perhaps we might consider tempering our exceptionalisms.
Yes, we may be unique on this earth as peak of development,
Does that claim that human beings are nature's ultimate?

Could other unknown intelligence evolving on other planets?
To my knowledge, cosmologists have not more than tenants.
With measures of humility may we earthly humans be cautious,
Might our inflated claims to omniscience be so preposterous?

The mysterious balances of being creatures of a Divine Creator,
Could avail limited human beings of realizing our Originator.
Yes, there are speculations by a few Scientists that we are unique,
Might that claim be feeding our needs to be creation's peak?

Where are the balances of humility within human investigator?
Are we becoming even more arrogant that claims no Creator?
The awareness of myths of creation long held by human beings,
Many cultures have encapsulated myths of Divine Creating.

These Transcendental Myths are beyond scientific investigations,
Science assumes that reality is measurable by homo sapiens.
These conflicts are energy that stimulates further exploration,
Roots of creativity presume living involves conflicting claims.

Our inquisitive brains stimulate our quest to discover even more,
Consequently, the natural effects are for us to further explore.
Without creative curiosity we'd be stuck in traditional answers,
Openly welcoming what could be also alternative responses.

PROVOCATIVE INTIMATIONS

These multiple possibilities provide us hypotheses to investigate,
Expanding our world of curiosity so that we might not inflate.
These realizations assume that we are open to other explanations.
Which could balance human beings from renegade generations.

Creative conflicts are important even though producing tensions,
This awareness can contribute to immense further extensions.
Learning about the unknown worlds are facets of our experience,
We can be grateful that there are unexplored more evidence.

Historically these types of creative conflicts are the usual norm,
What seems unusual is the contrast with tendencies to conform.
The pressures to avoid creative tensions are known in reflection,
Not surprisingly this is the energy about God in His Creation.

These realizations provide a context for what humanity is facing,
As history unfolds, the participants could find this embracing.

Creation is evolving with small steps that are included overall,
Our contributions are significant although considered small.

CASE STUDIES

Crises provide helpful case studies!
When confronting new realities!
Corporations may face bankruptcy
Some are threatened by failed history!

Illustrations from old industries
Iron-steel confront competitors!
Traditional retailers lose customers!
Competition provides lower prices!

Even Congregations have declined!
These are those called mainline!
New generations want inspiration!
Old liturgies now need re-generation!

Baptists, Methodists, Lutherans, Presbyterians!
Are weighted down by old their traditions!
In facing what is also contemporary
By not encouraging new creativity!

POSSIBILITIES

Re-generation may be possible!
New formats may be plausible!
Management layers can stagnate!
Discouraging bottoms-up to recreate!

New technologies may be included
Instead of new ideas being excluded!
Creative contributions are encouraged!
Stimulating old formats that are aged!

Letting go of over-worked programs
That repeats old ideas as standards!
Risking the possibilities of failures
Experiments are not all successes!

Encouraging inter-cultural layouts
Providing hospitality for immigrants!
Fostering a sense of global mission
Furthering Christ's Great Commission!

Risk-taking becomes very stimulating!
Consistent with original under-takings!
Congregations may benefit trying risks!
As a facet of becoming more creative!

JUSTICE AND ITS CONVERSE

Justice is held out as an ideal in many global cultures!
World Religions emphasize justice for being crucial!
Without a substantial degree of fairness, people fail,
Consequently, parameters of justice we should avail!

In America, we publicize justice to be for everyone!
But is this completely true when it comes to practices?
It is assumed that all people are equally protected!
But consider flagrant omissions are tilted backwards!

Laws are not equally enforced for both the rich and poor!
Enforcement of regulations varies so it not always sure!

Large corporate interests can violate laws repeatedly!
They can afford lawyers who know how to get by usually!

Shenanigans on Wall Street demonstrate unfair justice!
Their violations often appear to be seen as entitlements!
Rarely are wealthy thoroughly tried for their crimes!
Why do you think their political gifts have little shame?

Poor folks receive wide variations in even minor crimes,
Law enforcement officials make arrests many times!
The poor are accused and entitled to defense attorneys,
Frequently, second-rate lawyers defend them carelessly!

Advocacy for disenfranchised is encountered before judges,
They cannot afford expensive fees so they will then suffer!
Prosecution attorneys often are not rewarded for justice!
Defense attorneys quickly prepare to defend these cases.

DIFFERENTIAL JUSTICE

Justice differs for wealthy and persons in the bottom tiers,
Others may become victims of compromised witnesses!
Until recently, "line-ups" were inaccurately identified!
Under stress, witnesses are not reliable but pressured!

Accused declared guilty may serve 12-25 years in jail!
DNA testing finds gross errors withheld from defendants!
Prosecution attorneys may not share important data!
These practices are unjust when accused are found guilty!

When unfair trials convict an innocent person wrongly,
Individuals suffer plus families and even communities!
Texas and other states can onvict for guilt unfairly,
These wrongdoings are never undone sufficiently!

There are additional limitations even with fair justice!
These shortcomings are not readily acknowledged!
Justice is only one facet of fulfilling responsibilities,
Exploring these downsides reveal more culpabilities.

16. WHAT JUSTICE CANNOT ACCOMPLISH![48]

Justice has only limited preventive influence and power!
It rarely stops people doing terrible crimes to another!
Justice can identify transgressions and pass sentences,
It cannot restore, nor reconcile or make things better!

Justice is reactive to violations rather than proactive!
Until violations occur, justice systems are not involved!
Then they investigate, charge accused and prosecute!
But until a crime happens, justice is rather reclusive!

There are functions that justice systems do rightly!
Punishment prevents additional crimes by the guilty!
But prisons rarely rehabilitate inmates in their lives,
Often prisoners learn how to do even worse crimes!

So what is essential to complement limited justice?
Education is a very long-term process to socialize!
Religion also possesses an important key teaching,
So that humanity can effect even better correcting!

Societies that forget to forgive can never be truly just!
Forgiveness hopefully provides a corrective balance!
This may be very difficult for human beings to offer,
While forgiveness is central in the Christian Gospel!

---

[48] Wells, Samuel, April 17, 2013, "Forgiving Ahab: Naboth's Vineyard and God's Justice," Christian Century.

OLD TESTAMENT PUNISHMENT

The Old Testament provides lessons in punishment,
  The New Testament witnesses to what is ultimate!
I Kings 21 provide a vivid account of King Ahab crime!
  He was a dominating ruler creating havoc in his time!

While Ahab led Israel in defeating Ben-Hadad readily,
  But Ahab's arrogance is displayed to find him guilty!
He covets the prosperous vineyard of Naboth as owner,
  King Ahab's Queen Jezebel also wanted this garden!

Vegetables grew with Naboth's tending done carefully,
  So evil envy motivated King Ahab as jealous royalty!
While the vineyard was near the royal palace adjacently,
  But Naboth refused to relinquish what he had inherited!

False testimony was contrived that Naboth is guilty!
  Jezebel arranged that Naboth cursed God and King!
Scoundrels trumped up charges against his innocence,
  So Naboth was condemned followed by quick stoning!

When this crime had occurred, God instructed Elijah!
  As a faithful prophet, he confronted powerful Ahab!
Announcing where Naboth's blood, Abad would bleed!
  Ahab was condemned for jealousy and for murder!

Evil Jezebel was also condemned for her conspiracy,
  Elijah pronounced that dogs would eat her flesh!
Ahab's jealousy was provoked further by his Queen,
  Jezebel is notoriously known as a person who is evil!

NEW TESTAMENT FORGIVENESS!

Ahab and Jezebel symbolize humanity's weaknesses,
   But the New Testament has a Gospel of Forgiveness!
The sacrifice by God's Son, Jesus, provides hopefulness!
   In contrast to Old Testament accounts of punishment!

Consider the central message of forgiveness by Jesus!
   Justice is balanced with the Gospel for Forgiveness!
Jesus ministry prefigures this with helpful accounts!
   He forgives sins of those who would be condemned!

In Luke 7: 36-50, Jesus is in the house of a Pharisee!
   Simon is furious as a sinful woman washes Jesus' feet!
She bathes his feet with her tears and dries with her hair,
   But Simon is so angry about her magnanimous display!

Then Jesus turns the tables on Simon for being neglectful!
   He points out the rudeness of Simon that is multiple!
Jesus teaches there is only way to deal with wrongdoing,
   He announces that his new way is to be more forgiving!

Forgiveness does what justice cannot even accomplish!
   Why forgive? So that we do not react with bitterness!
Forgiveness is the most powerful energy in the Universe!
   This gift of Jesus provides the complement to justice!

In contrast to King Ahab's evil for the stoning of Naboth,
   Jesus is innocently tried by the establishment's justice!
Yes, Jesus is falsely charge, flogged and then crucified!
   "Father forgive them for they know not what they do!"

JUSTICE PLUS FORGIVENESS!

While human beings tout the very best of justice systems,
Often not realizing that even fair justice in very limited!
It cannot heal, restore or rehabilitate those who violate,
Justice provides revenge, punishment and incarcerates!

Forgiveness attempted by humans has its shortcomings,
Human beings cannot provide both healing and forgiving!
What is beyond human capabilities is met by the Gospels,
Jesus Christ provides us with both justice and forgiveness!

This does not mean that civil societies can neglect justice,
But rather to recognize the limits of its own effectiveness!
The contrast of two stories provide a glimpse of the Gospel,
Evil is humanly insurmountable! Forgiveness is available!

The Gospel discloses that justice and forgiveness are needed,
The contrast of King Ahab and Queen Jezebel is obvious!
Jesus' sacrificial crucifixion provides us with God's Love,
We are forgiven! We have hope! Plus Good News to share!

CONTEMPORARY CHALLENGES

"New Occasions Teach New Duties!"
Challenge countering old traditions!
Empowering dynamics with energy
Pursuing excitement and creativity!

Older generations need to adapt!
Then young are not handicapped!
Both Old & Young working together!
Jointly they will do so much better!

Older ones have experience and resources,
But the Younger possesses greater energy!
Together empowered into the future!
For mutual benefit in their culture!

Experience energized by imagination!
Balance both for producing creations!
Overcoming the inertia from stagnation
Providing a better future for celebration!

SPLENDOR

Conscious minds evolved miraculously!
With cognitive awareness and emotionally!
This human species has become amazing
Among our own gifts, our mind is precious!

Major intellectual achievements unfold!
Creative contributions in Arts and Sciences!
Civilizations develop by human minds!
Historical evidence plus current finds!

Cultures depend upon human resources!
Plus natural resources and opportunities!
Collective minds can become "multipliers!"
By encouraging teamwork to be creators!

RANGE OF DISPERSION

The most brilliant are known as "geniuses;"
Comprehending the difficult complexities.
By IQ measures, they are above 150 level!
Three standard deviations above normal!

The highest level of cognitive functions,
Educationally, can deal with abstractions!
Intellectually they are among the "elite!"
Ordinary problems are more concrete!

Lower IQ persons are also valuable!
Equally in need for being respectful!
Special Education is also most helpful!
To help persons express their potentials!

These persons also make their contributions!
By helping others to express appreciations!
That all typical be both thankful and joyful!
Genuine smiles help us all to be grateful!

They readily display emotional intelligence!
Tuning into personal feelings and belligerence!
This affective behavior rather than cognitive
Social and emotional intelligence is salient!

17. SPECIAL SEASONS FOR LIVING

This quartile of living presents us with challenges opportunities,
In "The Seasons of Human Life," we re-launch with springtime.
Then our chronological sequences:-summertime, fall and winter,
We human beings can pursue purpose and personal curiosities,

SPRINGTIME

In nature, life emerges in the spring with sprouts and activities,
New growth spurts forth out of the earth nesting proclivities.
Children get restless "to get out to do things" while unconfined,
Kids, animals, plants and birds innately know spring has emerged.

School children waffle restlessly with energy to be outdoors,
  Boys are eager to play ball, go fishing and swim on the shores.
Girls create their activities like biking to visit friends and families,
  Traveling to camp, plus tease boys who smaller until mid-teens.

Colorful imaginations stimulate youth in expansive experiences,
  Exploring, stretching their skills, widen readiness for adventures.
Mischief has both pros and cons that being troubles and successes,
  Self-directed play creates special skills plus new creative processes.

Springtime in life lays solid foundations upon which to grow,
  Planting seeds in this season with expectations about what to sow.
Protecting sprouts, watering and weeding, cultivating as humans,
  Siblings help, siblings fight, sibling rivalry of young men & woman.

SUMMERTIME

After rapid spurts of growth, launching from the nest is attempted,
  Slips and falls plus ups and downs are part of becoming developed.
Like eagles growing, flapping their wings, bodies are strengthened
  Minds and bodies, skills and falls accumulate as days lengthened.

Nature's Summer Parades draw up to engage in outdoor activities,
  Plants accelerate their beauty; Flowers attract the birds and bees.
Water invites us to jump in for cool swimming; lakes for fishing,
  Sailboats, glide through challenging waves of ocean's breaking.

"Going to Camp" excites adventurous youth but not all introverts,
  Friendship enriches and skills grow as we become natural experts!
Traveling and camping involve us into adventures into the unknown,
  Stories and photos refresh our favorite memories to be later shown.

FALL

Fall is a mixture of maturing harvests and also schools beginning!
   Days become shorter while fall colors come out with full bursting!
New classes and classmates expand us to engage our curiosities,
   Sports enlarge our physical coordination plus our dexterities.

In alternate year, campaigning for those seeking to serve in office,
   Candidates attempt to chance as attractive stars trying to entice.
Agricultural communities become excited about their harvesting,
   Numerous celebrations and holidays invite to engage in feasting!

Sports have full seasons for the World Series plus a football game,
   Teams display their talents, battling contests and search for fame.
Season of Thanksgiving are festive while Holidays are proclaiming,
   Families plan very special occasions for celebrating and sharing.

WINTER

Preparations anticipate long winter of hibernating and reclusions,
   Animals adapt their furs to be warmer, woollier than other seasons.
Storing up food for survival plus resting yearlong work and tensions,
   Festive celebrations, winterized dwellings plus holiday preparations.

Designated as year's end, winter is also for new expectant planning,
   Completing projects, paying taxes, plus advent season observing.
The seasonal cycles provide rhythm necessary for human renewing,
   Dormant seasons are actually very active for futures with hoping!

The Seasons of Life introduces human search for personal meaning,
   Jointly planning for the future year provides us new beginnings.
Cycles build up our capacities for new starts for enriched living,
   Spiraling into the future ahead calls us for greater energizing.

GIFTS AND TALENTS

We are encouraged to develop our own gifts!
Physical, mental, interpersonal to be curious!
Human beings value these unique qualities!
These gifts are also correlated with abilities!

St. Paul valued our human minds especially!
Suggested we "take on the mind of Christ!"[49]
Moreover, he cautions us to have humility!
So we have special appreciation for Divinity!

Our minds are invisible and essential!
In order to develop our own potential!
Education is best designed to do cultivation!
Use our minds constructively, not hesitation!

"IRREGULARITIES"

Our mind is equally sensitive as our body!
As injury and irregularities may also display!
Emotions can burden minds with depression!
Brain deformities may result in regression!

Human minds can also become corrupted!
Violence is expresses of being uncontrolled!
Psychopaths may do real violations of laws
Paranoia and schizophrenia may hear voices!

Cultures may develop distortions aggressively!
Revenge can be acted out by the very angry!
Hitler's grandiosity inflated his revengeful ego!
He corrupted his people to do murderous evil!

---

[49] New Testament, Philippians 2.

Recently ISIS had leaders with angry minds!
Expressing violent hostility to Western cultures!
Just how balanced are these various views?
They all want attention on global TV news!

SOCIOPATHIC CULTURES

But Hitler and ISIS were vicious dictators!
Mao in China eliminated his own millions!
Death registered in the tens of millions!
Civil Wars resulted from his terrorism!

Stalin's Russia experienced huge terrorism!
Many estimates are over thirty million!
The sociopathic dictators are horrendous!
Their pathological minds were duplicitous!

Leaders in Thailand and Myanmar are notorious!
Annihilating their people but also boisterous!
Cultural violence lets the choice of leaders!
These atrocious minds in military powers!

INTERACTIONS

Social interactions multiply contributions!
Small teams and large scale organizations!
These are complementary combinations!
By resulting in hybrid effective unions!

Geniuses can provide helpful inputs!
Plus larger scale work of cooperatives!
Both are essential for optimal results!
Interactions of all citizens really enriches!

Human cultures are engaged holistically!
Not monolithic but including polyistically!
Somewhat more super-naturalistically!
Beyond accurate measures statistically!

Our human minds do benefit from Biology
And equally significant grows out culturally!
These qualities generated by God's creativity!
Establishing many ingredients growing globally!

DID JESUS SING?

This message explores the occasions when Jesus may have sung,
Imagination is essential to hear the music once could have begun.
Certainly he cried as a baby that Mother Mary would call singing!
His cries may have not been all melodic, but this was a beginning!

Can you imagine as a boy he never would be involved in singing?
If he any friends at all, he would have had reasons for his joining.
At twelve years, did Jesus sing with his buddies while traveling?
His family on a pilgrimage to Jerusalem would naturally engaging.

Can you hear the walking music that kept friends to walk in line?
Camp songs on such a long trip would have involved singing time!
Did Jesus and his twelve disciples plus admiring women sing along?
Maybe they "warmed-up" the crowds that heard Jesus messages!

People can easily remember verses of Scriptures when they are sung,
Throughout human history, music and rhythmic forms did belong.
We have evidence that Jesus knew many Psalms that he repeated,
He remembered them very well that he spontaneously delivered.

The account of the Last Supper or Passover Meal expresses clearly,
After they finished their meal together, "they sang a hymn" gladly.

What hymn were they singing and what instruments were played,
This male chorus of twelve had Jesus as the leader who directed.

Choirs and organs included in their worship of prayers and praise.
Today liturgists would love to have access to Jesus' musical scores,
He likely incorporated music with engaging worship and <u>Psalms</u>.

While we do not have an air-tight case except singing after Supper,
To argue otherwise would label another person as a real Doubter.
So this an invitation to discover occasions when Jesus was singing,
There is ample evidence to affirm that Jesus in music was engaging!

CLINCHING EVIDENCE

Chorus:

> "Jesus Loves Me This I know!
> For He personally told me so!"
>
> "His assurance is best for you,
> <u>Bible</u> stories tell us 'tis true!"

Verses:
What more is there needed now about love?
Jesus comes down incarnating from above!
> *Chorus*

With His self-giving love connecting into us,
His Hope and Love, He is faithful and just!
> *Chorus*

Now is the finest time to compose this score,
Jesus sings his music right through us more!
> *Chorus*

Plus more instruments from a full orchestra,
His majestic symphony is abundantly extra!
Chorus

Now, all together let us sing this chorus again,
"Jesus Loves You and Me & also all Creation!"
Chorus

Jesus as Guru
By Nakedpastor David Hayward on Sep 06, 2016 08:11 am

V. CULMINATION

18. PROGNOSIS

Are we in the middle of how democracy is being manipulated in transition?
Many citizens are very slippery in their own views and expressed conviction.

Is our fragile democracy caught up in the middle of grave unnoticed danger?
Obviously there are vested interests of wealthy persons expressing anger.

Symptoms are often confused with the real causes of our hidden problem,
Are we preoccupied with our personal concerns but need more wisdom?

Democracy is a very fragile form of governance because it is so vulnerable,
To special interests of wealthy persons who hope the masses are gullible.

Incited fears from messages are often promoted to provide vivid distraction,
To protect their own selfish interests rather than supporting better action.

We are living in a gradual age of political transition advanced by wealthy,
Do you sense that our body politic is far from being considered healthy?

Awareness of problems is important in processes of proper identification,
Without accurate diagnosis we are not ready to act with the best solution.

Otherwise we really have diseases in our internal body politic as unnoticed,
Don't we need prevention of these illnesses before we are being exterminated?

Conscientious citizens perceive much more than their own special interest,
Responsible voters endorse candidates who advance what is socially best.

We need committed public officials who are motivated by servant leadership,
The persons to elect are both citizens and officials who work in partnership!

In the Pledge of Alliance to the flag of the United States is "UNDER GOD!"
To preserve our freedom, equality, democracy let us remember our word.

BECOMING

Near-Experiences have an impact on living;
For some it prompts their reason for being!
So they examine why they are now here;
Posing to them enlarging their careers.

These persons search for their own purpose;
Thereupon, their existence becomes a pursuit!
They explore for great compelling existence,
Refocusing how others notice their presence.

An enlarged set of reasons to be on Earth;
This exploration had not occurred since birth.
Their near-death opened up personal worth;
Discovering purpose that enlarges their "girth!"

Now their own life is very highly treasured;
Living becomes more than years measured!
Subjectively for them, even more is awaiting;
Existence enlarges into further "becoming!"

BEYOND CREATION OF THIS UNIVERSE

Science researches this Universe known as reality
While Science struggles to appreciate Theology!
Now efforts are models of conflict or compatibility;
Beyond Science and Theology are many mysteries!

As these fields of concern move toward maturity
There arise many paths toward fuller inquiry!
Both benefit from mutual respect and compatibility
As vast unknown hold humans from uncertainty!

Can we face that we have limited mentality?
In contrast to thinking "know-it-all humanity?"
To the emerging brain ascertaining reality?
Or are human brains much less than infinity?

Assumptions that creation is comprehensible
Inherently constricts other "phenomenologies!"
Are humans assuming the epitome of reality?
To this question heresy as not scientifically?

In Science and Mathematics, we consider unknowns
As we research for discovering even more knowns!
The human brain continues to be very mysterious
100 billion neurons with trillions of connections!

BRAIN INTRICACIES

Yes, more is comprehended than historically!
No, full comprehensions is still beyond humanity!
Discipline pursuits give awareness and consciousness.
We are still one on the surfaces of these inquiries!

Our consciousness continues to be a mystery!
Even among brain researchers scientifically!
Most analyses concerns immediate connections!
Micro- awaiting the macro-brain functions!

Can human beings go beyond our subjectivity?
Or is objectivity beyond our human inquiries?
New progressive hypotheses are very essential
For humanity to realize our limited potentials!

Humanity is progressively aware of our boundaries!
Or are we captive to our own human egocentricity?

Reflection may reveal our limited in comprehension
  Of the complexities that abound in this Creation!

Does empirical evidence show the whole Truth?
  Are factual data describing universal worth?
What multi-verses now have different laws?
  Will human comprehend that we have flaws?

TRUTH?

"The Truth" is a key curiosity of humanity!
  Does anyone comprehend this in societies?
Could "The Truth" be beyond our bodies?
  Beyond collective brains in this century?

Are humans capable of recognizing limits?
  Or should we consider ourselves as "ultimates?'
Are our brains able to reach truthful summits?
  Or is this also a peak within human arrogance?

Why are these questions every considered?
  Planting doubts about our human competence?
Who is the final arbiter about these disputes?
  Can rulings to be appealed "if anyone refutes?"

Are questions as important as the answers?
  Why does science continue to test hypotheses?
Future generations might question conclusions!
  Just like currently we reject past observations!

These ongoing quests will question our past?
  Scientific methodologies make room to recast!
So will humanity ever to able to understand
  The "Why's?" The Where's? The How's, When's?

GOD VS. VIOLENCE

With experience as a Nuclear Officer
    Then 55 years as a Christian Minister!
        Let me contrast these two experiences
        With personal observations and patience!
    Both have a direct focus upon power!
God's Power versus Nuclear Weapons!

Both are awesome for beholding!
    One is the Creator; other destroying!
        God is universal; Weapons controlling!
        God is delivering: Weapons do destroying!
    One is GOOD NEWS; other are bad news!
One is loving; But weapons need fearing!

Oh, yes, some Preachers preach fear!
    With threatening messages to hear!
        The Gospel is Good News! Other bad!
        Good News is hopeful; other is sad!
    Prayers Uplifting; weapons dread!
Both have POWER to characterize!

God's Good News is in Jesus Christ!
    Nuclear weapons are for sacrifice!
        One from the pulpit; other to ignite!
        One brings joy; other brings fright!
    Good News to deliver; other stored!
One is for the public; other locked!

God is Creative; Weapons Destructive!
    Gospel is for sharing; The other to be secret!
        God is Loving; Weapons are for testing!
    Good News is hopeful; Other harming!
Worship is reverent; Other for fearing!

Go out into the world; Other bombing!
One is a Calling; The other threatening!
One is spreading; The other terrorizing!
One is Theology; Other is Technology!
Gospel is glad; Bombs contaminating!
Steeples and Bells; Silos, Planes, Subbing!

One is spreading; other for controlling!
Proliferating; Treaties non-proliferating!
Preaching vs. Mutual Assured Destroying!
Gospel delivers; Bombs make suffering!
One is Divinity; The other for fearing!
One is a blessing; Other terrorizing!

How will humanity handle weapons?
In 75 years, have we learned lessons?
Will there ever be a nuclear holocaust?
How many more lives have to be lost?
"Come, now, let us reason together!"
To mutually discover to have it better!

Life hurts! The environment suffers!
Might we find peace for the future?
Humans invented nuclear weapons;
Can we discover future millenniums?
Violence begets even more violence!
Non-violence is for peacefulness!

UNCERTAINTIES

Yes, the human brain is an amazing organ!
Possibly the greatest of living organisms!
Does it qualify for knowing ultimate reality?
Is this question to be decided by humanity?

Advanced Sciences now encounter uncertainties!
Creation if filled with numerous complexities!
Currently science recognized many mysteries!
Waiting to be investigated with methodologies!

How extensive will the Universe ever expand?
So far, human awareness does not understand!
Is space endless without limited boundaries?
Mathematics already has the concept of infinity!

In time, will human brains grow to understand?
Who can now investigate to discover an answer?
Scientific technological methods are challenged;
How to design verification with research studies?

Are there issues that confront our limitations?
Now time, this question provides consternation!
Now human knowledge is certainly amazing!
But how extensive will it continue growing?

CELEBRATION OF MEANING

Why is personal meaning so attractive?
Is this an experience especially positive?
To curious persons meaning is essential
To pursue their own lifetime potential!

People with purpose often thrive
Wanting to reach what while they live!
Meaningful purpose does empower
Helping one's life to climb up higher!

Meaning does enhance our living!
So that receiving becomes giving!

Investing oneself to be worthwhile
To let loving others becomes a style!

Meaning is also very inspiring!
Lifting up one's purpose for living!
Life then becomes more hopeful
Eventually becoming consequential!

PERMA

Yes, personal meaning is important;
Meaning helps us feel significant!
PERMA abbreviates these effects

P-----Positive Emotions
E-----Engagement
R-----Relationships
M-----Meaning
A-----Achievement

CHANGING DIETS

The transition from hunting to farming
Has fattened humans when eating.
Humans ate more fruits and berries,
Slimmest resulted with fewer calories.

Hunters consequently were slimmer,
Walking, stalking and running.
Their muscles were conditioned
With much less fatty nutrition.

When farming became established,
Livestock were also then fattened.
The beef, pork and also mutton,
Has been consumed to be gluttons.

Yes, farming is very hard work,
To plow, plant, cultivate, harvest!
Town and city people eat heavily,
Adding pounds of weighty calories.

Soil has become over-worked;
Annuals and bi-annuals harvested.
After many years, soil is depleted,
Even when also richly fertilized.

Moreover, more water is required,
For the crops to be then raised.
Irrigation makes water depleted
For thirsty groups when heated.

Animals raised from birth to slaughter,
Do consume large volumes of water.
Nature does not always provide rain,
So rivers, ponds and lakes are drained.

Now entrepreneurs have better ideas.[50]
Now claiming to produce foods better.
Creating meals from cells is a petri dish.
And growing lettuce in skyscrapers.

Over 100 experts warn about exploitation.
When using land and water for nutrition.
If populations grow to 9.7 billion by 2050
Traditional farming will have difficulties.

---

[50] Semuels, A., February 3, 2020, "Finding a Changing World," <u>TIME.</u>

Mission-driven to find new technology
Proteins like fish and meat from cells!

"Vertical farming" to raise vegetables!
Producing greens at multiple levels.

Lab-grown protein for hamburgers!
Producing nutrients in "bioreactors!"
"Exo Crickets" as a protein source,
Now are sold by modern growers.

Peas, mung beans and fava beans,
Processed to produce sausages!
"Huel" makes powders and drinks
To provide nutrition as equivalent.

Protein derived from thin air,
By using microbial fermentation.
Resembling wheat derived from water
Flour from water, nutrients and carbon.

Agricultural changes help climate change,
From 21 to 37% of greenhouse emissions.
Food security mitigating climate changes,
Water saved and environment protected.

Can humans increase with less?
Researchers are doing their best.
Plant-based eating not from animals,
Could be produced by food giants!

BY-PRODUCTS

A by-product expresses true happiness!
  Even when experiencing restlessness!
Energy become definitely is uplifting
  As happiness truly enhances meaning!

Hope draws up to get our ahead!
  It lifts us to rise up to get out of bed!
Our days become full of expectations!
  Makes personal meaning a celebration!

Meaning is intangibly an inspiration!
  Meaning may not be a direct target!
Meaning often arises as a by-product!
  It can draw us forward to go onward!

Likewise we rarely would be cold
  To making a birthday to be our goal!
Rather birthdays are celebrated!
  Happening to help us feel elated!

Dreaming adds even more to memories!
  Day-dreaming plus our night reveries!
Dreams just happen to be uncontrolled
  May compel us to become more bold!

SIGNIFICANCE!

Significance can be mesmerizing!
  This should not at all be surprising!
Inspiring us with a reason for being!
  Plus enriching us personally for living!

Hoping is clearly very beneficial!
Hope draws us ahead to potentials!
Love that is hopeful is so inherent!
Drawing us upon our deepest roots!

As we search for personal meaning
Life likewise becomes fascinating!
Looking forward is very enhancing
Providing energy for worthy living!

Our meaning calls for celebrating!
It is contagious for others waiting!
Inspirations arise to go on further
Drawing us on our path forward!

18. SOLIPSISM

What is the meaning of this puzzling word?
Does "sol" suggest a term about "The Sun?
Indirectly, this question makes connections
Suggesting what "rotates around us humans!"

Solipsism psychologically parallels egocentrism
Epistemologically, it connotes human subjectivism!
Metaphysically the self includes only the present
Past and future are excluded as states relevant!

The "Self" knows exclusively its own perception!
"Self" is considered that center of the Universe!
Everything else shall then rotate around me!
One's own perspective advocates egocentrism!

Do our scientific orientations see "solipsism?"
As if Science is the sole type of verification?

Will "solipsistic" Science be aware of limits?
  Or are "The Truths" expressed by Metaphysics?

Metaphysics considers Ontology and Epistemology!
  "How?" and "Being" now do we know full reality?
Our own human brain power is just one source!
  Other realms of knowing included in course!

"BEYONDERING!"

This term may now be briefly comprehended:
  "Beyond what we humans have predicted!"
Beyonders go further than ever expected!
  From early forecasts that were outed!

Expressed in hypotheses of multi-verses!"
  We have evidence of billions of galaxies!
Each with millions of suns and planets!
  What might be other expanses of realities?

Solipsism is insufficient for us to appreciate
  Many solar systems would be expansive!
Beyond narrow self-centered perspectives
  So that this solar system is one elective!

"The Music of the Spheres" is boundless!
  Beyond the realms of just one Universe!
Creation by Divine Power is so inclusive!
  Countering narrow scope to be exclusive!

Augustine recognized "Our Souls are Restless!"
  "Until we eventually find our rest in Thee!"
He possessed awareness of Greek Philosophy
  Was influenced by Aristotle's methodology!

IMMORTALITY<>TEMPORALITY

This contrast strikes at the core of human-Divine encounters,
   Only a few cultures have maintained that they are immortal!
Vast civilizations recognize the termination of human life,
   Recognizing that all living creatures of earth will also die!

This realization that "Being" for humans does reach limits,
   Compared with existence beyond Time and Space of Divinities!
To be aware of mortality is a key experience to acknowledge,
   So that temporary living creatures only continue as privileged!

The Monotheistic Traditions convey awareness of our mortality,
   Judaism, Islam and Christians include this in their Theology!
That Divinity is Eternal outside of creations Time and Space,
   Providing for guidelines for living while existing on this Earth!

Awareness of mortality imprints upon humans with variety:
   One dismal response is then to give in to this eventuality.
Such resignation is often expressed in fatalism in "Non-Being,"
   So then Non-Being dominates this outcome is unsurprising.

An opposite viewpoint involves assuming one lives forever,
   Such assumptions are protected from the human endeavors.
Both of these polar opposites have proponents to propose,
   That these understandings of creation may be erroneous!

Another persistent set of responses involves animate beings,
   Each species comes into existence with different genetics.
There are species that are without any conscious awareness,
   Seemingly, these creatures are born, live and not persist!

Beings with a Neuroscience brains that are sufficiently large,
   May develop recognition of their beginning and their ending!

Awareness of birth and death is observed in various species,
   While there is only limited research on the others' insights!

When a member of a mortal species realizes they will die,
   There are noticeable responses that are communicated outside.
Elephants and horses provide the sense of mortal empathy,
   Plus additional species with various expressions of sympathy!

This poem is designed primarily to focus on human realizations,
   With our own limited temporal insights are derived from creation.
Consequently, attention is given to traditional sets of responses,
   With the purposes for identifying research under these conditions.

COMPETITION VS. COOPERATION

These contrasting reactions include both strength and weaknesses,
   Suggesting those valuable qualities that might be encouraged!
This poetry will first consider individual type of our responses,
   There will be consideration of social actions of civilizations.

Propensities for rivalry is obvious when observations are made;
   Animal behavior reveals rival actions by both males and females!
Stalking males typically show behaviors to dominate their females,
   With ceremonious practices expressing their prowess of dominance.

Darwin provided observations known as "Survival of the Fittest!"
   Thereby suggesting that dominant males try their protectiveness!
This scientific conclusion supports "Competition vs. Cooperation!"
   Simplifying complex behaviors into social and individual actions!

The propagation of species is the result of this instinctiveness,
   Elegantly explaining the crass biological strategy for existence!
For over 150 years this hypothesis prevails about reproduction,
   Plus survival of the most fit to cope with nature in competition!

Evolutionary research projects have confirmed this hypothesis,
The elegance of this principle appeals to scientific researchers.
Very few challenges have survived that are tested empirically,
Only limited refinements have been incorporated eventually.

However, there are suggestions from scientific research as refined,
That competitive fitness is one facet of these traditional findings.
Consequently, the next section will take careful time to consider,
Variations which are increasingly prominent in animal behavior!

Both among living animal species and also in human behavior,
An issue challenges the competitive explanations among creatures.
This refining hypothesis is being increasingly pervasive in research,
Suggesting cooperative behavior may prevail over being competitive.

E.O. Wilson[51] assesses old longitudinal research from the vertebras,
This variation is gaining attention while it is being evaluated.
Wilson challenges traditional concepts of selfishness vs. altruism,
With over 50 years of empirical research, he finds supportive.

The specifics of his conclusions can be reviewed in literature,
So that different conclusions may then also become evaluated.
Wilson also extrapolates beyond animal to human behavior,
Offering provocative hypotheses that will now be investigated.

Investigators need to research Wilson's unusual new hypotheses,
If not, there may be inconclusive confusion continuing otherwise!

Assuming that his recent formulations have validity to consider,
Following concepts are submitted to evaluation by researchers.

---

[51]   Wilson, E.O., 2012, The Social Conquest of Earth, W.W. Norton and Company, Ltd.

SPECIES PLUS INSTITUTIONS

Human institutions are posited as similar to the human species,
 Due to phenomena as also the creations of mortal human beings.
There is extensive evidence that people see firms as eternal,
 But in reality, organizations develop from creation as terminal.

Consider religious institutions that are concerned with eternity,
 Are these human organizations immortal or are they terminal?
As an example, The Roman Catholic Church is 2000 years,
 Even Rome is considered the Eternal City upon seven hills!

How do you consider recently increasing evidence for mortality?
 Is this Church assuming to be divine rather than temporality?
Is this long-lasting institution deceptively pretending immortality?
 Other denominations seem to assume their very own infinity!

Or consider corporations that are licensed to exist by states,
 Most have less than one century of history for existence!
Yet, does it become apparent that these firms are immortal?
 Without realizing their creation not by Divinity but by humans!

Very few new corporations last two years as viable institutions,
 Participants quickly are aware of the mortality of corporations!
The demise by bankruptcy or dissolution are quickly forgotten,
 People do not want to remember these fragile organizations!

Extrapolating from the animate species to human organizations,
 Wilson's hypotheses offer scintillating concepts for consideration.
He suggests cooperation among species is essential for humans,
 Because competition pushed to extreme is selfishly destructive.

His research reveals that species enduring longitudinally for ages,
 Develop key patterns of species cooperation not competitiveness.

Competition has a destructive destiny for only winners to survive,
While cooperation provides altruistic behaviors to stay alive.

Wisdom derived from this model is significant for mortal beings,
Is competition an optimal instinct to overcome friend and enemies?
Consider what the outcome of ultimate competition might become,
If competitors are extinguished, what are the final consequences?

"The last person standing!" receives considerable attention now,
But consider the consequences of wiping everyone else out!
Is this the goal of human destiny that is recognized as mortal?
Is this the unrealized goal that is temporarily seen as victory?

NATIONS AS HUMAN INSTITUTIONS

Consider global affairs now while also considering History;
Could the last nation standing be the destiny of humanity!
The un-assumed outcome of national competition is to prevail,
As the triumphant nations over all others trying to succeed!

Parallel to the last person standing is the last nation to win,
What is there left of creation? Is this human's final limit?
Interaction with diverse cultures would not be every present,
Because only the winners could determine future existence!

An example, consider the dilemma of European nations today,
These nations have been defined by boundaries since 1648.

The Peace of Westphalia prescribed boundaries of future nations,
Then cultural languages and practices functioned side by side!

Rivalries were incipient immediately after the "Thirty Years War!"
The nations had competitive rivalries so unity was not restored.

Internal civil wars plus struggles between nations became evident,
When colonization occurred, competition motivated expansions.

The warring nations of Europe imposed rule upon other people,
The colonial powers dominated Africa, South America and Asia.
Exploiting people and resources of cultures in other continents,
Becoming causal reasons for later wars for their independence.

The competitive nature of national powers obviously prevailed,
The cultures in other continents became the victims quickly.
Of course, the powerful rich had enticing gifts to give out,
But these had unexpressed consequences as their subjects!

Armies were already known in these vulnerable weak cultures,
So they immediately acquiesced as over whelmed with powers.
But in a century or two of exploitation, resentments developed,
Expelling these colonial rulers known as Wars of Independence!

The history of the last 100 years provides terrible exploitation,
In Europe, two World Wars were declared that included Asia.
These destructive conflicts resulted in violent consequences,
Lessons from these devastating wars prompted inquiries.

Could the nations of the world find peaceful organizations?
Or would competitive conquests be the natural outcomes?
Attempts in the past century are temporary experiments;
Gradually, global humanity is discovering success and limits.

These are predicates that may be essential for motivation,
As only a limited remnant are asking the best questions.
How can humanity survive destructive competitiveness now?
Do human species have capacities in order for survival?

LESSONS TO BE LEARNED!

The crises of past millennia has been overlooked by many,
    Yet, there is a remnant of a few who are also visionary!
You are best advised this writer is a Professor with ideas,
    He is a visionary idealist who also imagines better futures.

Is creation having destinies to be self-destructive eventually,
    Or does this humanity have essential creative capacities?
How can people learn to optimize their qualities of creativity?
    Take Europe as a pilot study for all of human nationalities!

How can the traditional national culture of Europe cooperate?
    Economically these countries are now challenged to create.
Will their obstinate cultural pride and competitiveness prevail?
    If they are mutually destructive, is this the end of European?

Survival is an ominous threat that instills fear of continuing,
    Yes, fear is very motivating to find better problem solving.
So the threat of extinction as distinct cultures force choices,
    How can they overcome their ominous economic crises?

Will traditional models of competition provide better answers?
    Or can they find cooperative solutions for all to survive?
Pride and hatred have motivated Europeans for centuries!
    Will these nations self-destruct because of old enmities?

Inherently creative conflicts challenge humanity to improve,
    Without these motivations, little occurs except being stubborn.
With the ominous vision of demise from history as cultures,
    Will Europeans discover compromises for mutual benefits?

Conflicts contain dynamics to change by being transformative,
    That is an ominous realization to confront to become creative!

Can these old rival nations find avenues to be interdependent?
 Yes, they have already experimented with the Euro for finance!

But now they may be required to form an entity for survival,
 While their experiment has potential for wider globalization!
Can these old cultures face the fact that they are also mortal?
 Otherwise, if their assumption is eternity, they are less vital!

Resilience under enormous stress will be their test of endurance,
 Can separate nations find another model for interdependence?
This is a pilot model that should consider the United States,
 By overcoming differences and competition, states cooperate!

Moreover, the implication for the European challenge is major,
 Without finding good solutions, the rest of world is endangered.
Even rivalries of many millennium challenge global countries,
 But they might become more tolerant when under pressures.

What will help human cultures to discover better relationships?
 Will human competitiveness defeat alternatives of partnerships?
Humanity is amazingly adaptive when under survival conditions,
 This realization broadly sets the stage for making adjustments.

19. REALITY OF MORTALITY

Human beings and their created institutions also have limits,
 These mortal creations are not eternal or ever-enduring.
When this reality is recognized, then termination is faced,
 Prompting human deciders to deal with their termination!

To endure, human beings and their institutions must adapt,
 This realization confronts deciders to make better choices.
A few may ignore this reality by denying their own mortality,
 While the others may become aware of needs for creativity.

Creative conflict is a dynamic that motivate and also inspires,
   Possibilities are considered within the parameters of realities.
While God's Kingdom is eternal, human kingdoms are terminal,
   Making for necessities that cooperation helps recognize mortal.

Human beings facing mortality have wide ranges of responses,
   We extrapolate into the future as if we persist as immortals.
"Denial may prevail temporarily" while soon limitations exist.
   With this realization, there is readiness to learn otherwise.

Only God's Kingdom is Permanently Immortal for us to realize,
   This Kingdom is outside of the creation with Time and Space!
"Spacelessness and Timelessness" are beyond our comprehension,
   When one description is "That everything is right Here & Now!"

This awareness contributes to understanding finite and infinite,
   We are finite while God is Infinite beyond our human grasp!
When these realizations sink into our human consciousness,
   Then there is deeper cognizance of our own human finiteness.

Naturally becoming aware of these limitations is a challenge,
   Contributing to possible realizations of grave human limitations.
Consequently, the knowledge that we as human have mortality,
   May contribute to our appreciation of God's Own Immortality!

MYSTERIES OF LIFE AND DEATH

As a minister, I officiate at both wedding and funeral services,
   While Psychology provided supplements to Theological insights.
But the most profound life and death learning then occurred,
   My lst wife, Arlys developed Rheumatoid Arthritis in middle age.

She retired from her teaching at 45 as her frame weakened,
   Her deformities were awesome to notice while she was pained.

Numerous top-notch medical treatments did not arrest it,
   Eventually, her nine hospitalizations were death threatening.

Fortunately, Susan and Greg were both young adults in years;
   But none of us were aware of the learning that would occur.
Arlys was very near death during three emergency episodes,
   We had to face horrendous decisions during her prime age.

She courageously let me to engage in educational seminars,
   She had to face debilitation physically but never spiritually!
I was able to go for brief tours into Europe professionally,
   In 1980, 1982, and 1984 while she was suffering physically.

In 1986, I arrested preparing in New York for Soviet Union,
   She courageously faced episodes of further deterioration.
These experiences of knowing my wife was very threatened,
   Challenged my physical, emotional and spiritual resources.

Having known each other for over 45 years since childhood,
   She was very realistic about suffering that she withstood.
I learned more in this "Valley of Death" than ever before,
   Only faith plus energy could help me to keep on teaching.

Among hospital, home and classroom were responsibilities,
   Susan, Greg, Pastor, Colleagues kept me going these months.
Never had I learned so profoundly realities of life and death,
   Then after three week unconscious coma, she terminated!

I was exhausted but finished grading tests for that term,
   While I write these verses, tears are flowing down my face!
Never before with four degrees and 24 years as a minister,
   Had I experienced such deep grief challenging my Faith.

The "Valley of Death" became lonely and also devastating,
   She died without pain after ten years that were painful.

At 54, we were grandparents of a beautiful granddaughter,
This was Arlys' climactic experience of her life on earth.

For both sets of as Grandparents, we were amazed!
"Kari Beth" has the beautiful red hair that is a blazed!
Other Grandfather quickly exclaimed: "She's a Keeper!"
Among fishermen, "this catch" is the big convincer!

Her faith and humor nobly continued until unconsciousness,
As her primary supporter, the gap she left was notorious.
I finished an academic term; she finished an earthly course!
This led to grieving and also to a sense of unexpected relief.

Preparatory grieving had been occurring for years before,
I was unbelievably amazed how long her body endured.
In three-weeks of brain death, she eventually terminated.
Both my children held me up for the two funeral services!

Academic or professional experiences never prepared me,
I was letting go of a dear loved one who died with grace.
It had been my privilege to be her mate in life and death,
With vast professional experience, this was a key test.

My sister and brother plus mother-in-law were helpful,
Along with my children, Minister and friends, I endured.
At 54, I was an unexpected Widower who felt lonely,
Recalling these experiences is both painful and joyful.

Many persons have to let go of a dear loved one in life,
Until this occurs, the reality of death is unexpressed.
Writing these lines is only a scant reflection of grieving,
Fortunately, the unknown future was more relieving!

The Valley of Death is not experienced ourselves alone,
We have Our Shepherd who helps us face this together!

Walking through this Valley personally awaits each one,
With our Shepherd guiding us, we will never have fear!

A few weeks later, I felt myself shutter while grieving;
Pent up emotions stored up while I was preparing.
Yes, "letting go" was very important humanly to do;
These experiences helped me to then later renew.

RE-BEGINNING

Family, Faith and Friends become very significant;
Grieving experiences find them humanly important.
Yes, our personal relationships are seen as fragile;
We do rediscover that we only live for a while!

Our human bodies have many precarious limitations;
Fore-bearers have known this in religious traditions.
This awareness fosters cultivation of human religions.
Conveying to adherents that our lives are in transitions.

Yes, we as humans learn to adapt to so many changes;
Transformations are important to make adaptations.
Locally, Nationally and Internationally changes come;
Right now we have a new year that has just begun!

Democracies provide for transitions in our leadership;
We learn anew that voting is critical in citizenship.
As voters, we exercise very important responsibilities;
Electing our leaders who do introduce possibilities!

SHIFTING FOCUS

How will this big nation manage leading to keep afloat?
Should all unprepared citizens be expelled on next boat?
Exporting cheap labor is an unworkable policy for leaders,
Importing only informed/educated healthy immigration!

American educational quality has been steadily declining,
Teenagers are not qualifying in math, science and writing.
There are many explanations that each one is contributing,
The multiple causes of failure are essential for examining.

Have schools readily become child care and holding centers?
Have brilliant graduates gone into more lucrative careers?
Educators are the scapegoat of many critics who do unleash,
How effective are businesses measuring success and failures?

Do politicians and business managers master teaching skills?
Are solutions foisted on teachers also measure intangibles?
Why does the pay scale for teachers stay low in moderation?
Why so few lobbyists cannot do better education legislation?

Are parents and families really showing interest in education?
Has family life deteriorated so that parents show hesitation?
When families and communities do not have big expectations,
Big workloads, video games, and also television distractions.

Athletics can command more attention than school progress,
With high expenditures kids engage what is cool to regress.
Unhealthy diets and no exercise create problems of obesity,
Now over twenty-five percent are not qualified for military.

When legislative financing is given only limited priority,
The future of youth and nation limits national security.

Rising nations emphasize the important of good education,
America is slipping rapidly in declining future generation.

Our nation's greatest assets for success are human resources,
Yet we spend exorbitant budgets on elderly and arm forces.
Our national priorities are skewed in wasted investments,
Competing powers have superior human achievements!

Higher achieving in graduate education are a prime assets,
But being first motivates competitors endorse mindsets.
When other societies educate students as equally effective,
We may find too late where our education is defective.

WHAT IS OUR HOPE?

Changes are Happening!

Contemporary political games try to grab media attention,
Extravagant claims and bold showmanship on television.
The issues identified have shallow analysis of problems,
The simpler the presentation, the higher ratings become.

Until voters see what is missing we will not notice gaps,
Most people only see the surface coverage by their saps.
Television has changed the quality of politics and education,
In depth analysis is far too complicated to hold attention.

The more we elect controlling, uncreative public officials,
Then less innovative measures will become legislated.
They collectively juggle budgets to serve special interest,
Education will more likely to lack vision for guidance.

But if visionary innovators give priorities to the future,
There is more hope for rising generations to mature.

Tough candidate evaluations give education priority,
   While good- old-boy candidates will defend their party.

Educated and informed voters are keys in democracy,
   They will vote for qualified in educated candidacy
So efforts are important to constantly inform voters,
   Who will elect best officials, not only show-boaters.

America's adaptability is now surviving a showman;
   His narcissism has been pre-occupied with media.
While many citizens have been fascinated by him
   Voters have shown we do need a new transition.

If we can eliminate former tendencies to mindlessness.
   Then our youth will battle to overcome poor blindness.
This agenda requires determination and great vision,
   America will then become tops in world competition!

GOD'S GIFT, NOT OUR MEANINGLESS TALK

When does our talk have meaninglessness?
   And when is our own chatter meaningful?
      Paul suggests to those who teach the law;
      He helps us know law alone is a flaw!

Yes, law helps to guide our behavior;
   But the law alone is not our Savior!
Law sets guidelines for our own actions
But the law alone is not our salvation!

God's merciful graciousness redeems us?
   We have salvation by our God's Grace![52]
   We humans are saved by Christ's Sacrifice,
      Not by our own earnings to pay the price!

---

[52]   I Timothy 1: 6-7.

God hopes we accept His best gift;
We celebrate Christmas for this "lift!"
This Gift God is given especially for us!
We frequently state "IN GOD WE TRUST!"
Good News: Grace! Gratitude! Global!

"Good News" is the term for Gospel!
Expressing God's Grace to His People!
This hope is designed to overcome evil!
Revealing God's Incarnation in Jesus!
Entering Time and Space as a child!
Expressing His Divine Presence!

Both Divine & human, Jesus exists!
In all the past & present He persists!
Gracious God is also Eternally Present!
Sacrificing His Son in His Crucifixion!
Raising from death by Resurrecting!
Sharing Good News for all humanity!

Humanity's Hope calls for Gratitude!
Inviting people to express thanksgiving!
Acknowledging God's Gift in our living!
Appreciating forgiveness for our sinning!
Good News is designed for sharing!
To bring the Gospel to the living!

Good News is to be shared globally!
Intended worldwide with humanity!
With brothers and sisters in God's Family!
Christian communities' responsibility!
Called to share Good News globally!
Expressing Hope and Joy to humanity!

20. MEANING FOR QUALITY LIVING

Sources of Meaning

Meaning in living often occurs in strong marriages!
When partners are important then meaning derives!
Both positive and negative emotions mutually thrive!

If persons have purpose in living, by-products occur!
Meaning includes fulfillments, satisfaction and rewards!
Pleasure occurs in relations, work and being stewards!

A side effect of important pursuit is meaningfulness!
Setbacks, illness and failures are major challenges!
Dedication to major purposes is important pursuits!

Meaning persists in positive and negative experiences!
Investing energy and times plus valuable resistance!
Meaninglessness is important to discover happiness!

HAPPINESS<>MEANING

Both happiness and meaning are positive terms!
As human beings, we typically value these words!
Each is distinctive when together venturing forward!

Happiness is associated with optimism and joy!
Emotionally, we are happy doing what we enjoy!
Each is distinctive while together we move forward!

Meaning is also personal with different derivation!
Subjectively, meaning is more cognitive than emotion!
Both are "by-products" pursuing a purposeful mission!

Often one pursuit in life is to discover a mate!
In optimal matching, this is not considered fate!
Mutuality is valued in finding this marital state!

In relationships, persons may want to be happy!
Expectation of continued happiness is very tricky!
If happiness is a primary goal, marriage can be iffy!

A famous marriage psychiatrist[53] advises otherwise,
Disappointment is likely in marriage experiences!
Meaningful relations are more likely to enhance!

Since marital demands have disappointments!
Continued happiness is nearly an impossible intent!
Cycles of sadness and happiness are very realistic!

Meaning in living often occurs in strong marriages!
When partners are important then meaning derives!
Both positive and negative emotions mutually thrive!

If persons have purpose in living, by-products occur!
Meaning includes fulfillments, satisfaction and rewards!
Pleasure occurs in relations, work and being stewards!

A side effect of important pursuit is meaningfulness!
Setbacks, illness and failures are major challenges!
Dedication to major purposes is important pursuits!

Meaning persists in positive and negative experiences!
Investing energy and times plus valuable resistance!
Meaninglessness is important to discover happiness!

---

[53] Gugenbuhl-Craig, A.,

LIMITS OF HAPPINESS

If happiness is primary, disappointments occur!
Yes, happiness is joyful, but not as an only goal!
Life inherently includes both suffering and joy!

Persons can experience meaning while suffering!
Not as a goal but a realistic awareness in living!
Reflective persons with purpose may find meaning!

When unhappiness happens, it is typically troubling,
Negative experiences may become very depressing!
A more fulfilling pursuit is the search for meaning!

Frankl[54] gave profound insights in depressing situations!
A Nazi prisoner of war, he kept focused on expectations!
He accredited both maintaining hope in deep relations.

Quality living has key meaning!
Characterized what is fulfilling!
Plus experiences of significance!
That personally have importance!

Meaning makes life worthwhile
Providing a person unique style!
Meaning is internalized within!
Indirectly shown in relating!

Personal autonomy is primary!
Revealed in one's singularity!

Specialness in our personality
No one else has individually!

---

[54]   Frankl, V., Man's Search for Meaning

Even suffering has meaning!
  Finding ourselves reflecting!
  Life has both joys and sorrows!
Tough time has unhappiness.

Without meaning is a void
  As our experiences are bad!
  We learn from feeling sad
We can value what is glad!

We become aware of death!
  Living helps us feel worth!
  Supportive sources do help
Both human and also Divine!

Quality surpasses quantity!
  Meaning provides internality!
  Inside us is our own depth
Each one's intangibility!

Meaning is not a commodity
  It is not bought or sold!
  Meaning helps young and old
Valuing us to feel happy!

Each has personal experiences
  Providing us with significance!
  To God, we all have importance!
Enriching us with essence!

We all possess specialness!
  Contributing to our potential!
  Discovering is so essential!
Unfolding our uniqueness!

RESILIENCE

From Tragedies to Hopeful Resilience

What are the special dynamics to respond to tragedies?
How can hardy people handle these setbacks positively?
Can persons prepare to constructively address stresses?
Or are humans destined to consider life with fatefulness?
This message struggles with frequent human setbacks

Attempting to discover strategies when tragedy attacks.
Most heartbreaks are very unpredictable as surprises,
Catching us unprepared with the onset of these crises.

Common wisdom persists that we expect just very few,
Taxes are one and other is death, a cliché that is not new!
Such a limited perspective is so fatalistically anticipated,
Resigning many persons do not know about alternatives.

SEARCHING

Bhutan is a very a small country in the Himalayas!
They created the GHP—"Gross Happiness Product!"
This index expresses their own continuous search!

Meaning and happiness are not guaranteed in living!
Relationships and social involvements are inviting!
Our own personal values are crucial in searching!

What is important to us becomes very significant!
Work, involvements and relationships all enhance!
Investing attention and energy creates experiences!

Feeling worthless is notoriously an empty emotion!
Helping people find meaning is a crucial mission!
Investment in other persons becomes meaningful!

When we help persons become important they thrive!
They may discover significance for why they are alive!
Our own purpose in life may contribute how to thrive!

HAPPINESS<>MEANING

Both happiness and meaning are positive terms!
As human beings, we typically value these words!
Each is distinctive when together venturing forward!

Happiness is associated with optimism and joy!
Emotionally, we are happy doing what we enjoy!
Each is distinctive while together we move forward!

Meaning is also personal with different derivation!
Subjectively, meaning is more cognitive than emotion!
Both are "by-products" pursuing a purposeful mission!

Often one pursuit in life is to discover a mate!
In optimal matching, this is not considered fate!
Mutuality is valued in finding this marital state!

In relationships, persons may want to be happy!
Expectation of continued happiness is very tricky!
If happiness is a primary goal, marriage can be iffy!

Since marital demands have disappointments!
Continued happiness is nearly an impossible intent!
Cycles of sadness and happiness are very realistic!

LIMITS OF HAPPINESS

If happiness is primary, disappointments occur!
Yes, happiness is joyful, but not as an only goal!
Life inherently includes both suffering and joy!

Persons can experience meaning while suffering!
Not as a goal but a realistic awareness in living!
Reflective persons with purpose may find meaning!

When unhappiness happens, it is typically troubling,
Negative experiences may become very depressing!
A more fulfilling pursuit is the search for meaning!

Frankl[55] gave profound insights in depressing situations!
A Nazi prisoner of war, he kept focused on expectations!
He accredited both maintaining hope in deep relations!

SEARCHING

Bhutan is a very a small country in the Himalayas!
They created the GHP—--Gross Happiness Product!
This index expresses their own continuous search!

Meaning & happiness are not guaranteed in living!
Relationships and social involvements are inviting!
Our own personal values are crucial in searching!

What is important to us becomes very significant!
Work, involvements and relationships all enhance!
Investing attention and energy creates experiences!

---

[55] Frankl, V., <u>Man's Search for Meaning</u>

Feeling worthless is notoriously an empty emotion!
Helping people find meaning is a crucial mission!
Investment in other persons becomes meaningful!

When we help persons become important they thrive!
They may discover significance for why they are alive!
Our own purpose in life may contribute how to thrive!

BEYONDER-MENTS

Let me de-mystify BEYONDER-MENTS!
This idea is related to WONDER-MENTS!
It is derived from the adverb "BEYOND!"
Which is also connected to "WONDER!"
Poetically, we "wonder" and also reflect!
Prayerfully, we wonder about "beyonder!"

Beyonder infers visions which we wonder!
Beyonders are persons who go further!
Further than we ordinarily imagine!
We might connect these to "Evangel!"
This takes us to the realm of good news!
Trying to comprehend more of God's views!

God stretches us to envision "beyondering!"
To suggests mysteries beyond wondering!
God promises that we will have eternal life!
Which is beyond the limits of earthly strife!
For a "BEYONDERING-MOMENT" here & now!
Prayerfully close your eyes & let your head bow!

Focus upon what heaven may mean to you!
"Beyonder-Moments" will help us renew!
Beyond here and now to there and then!

Permit your imagination to then venture!
Now let you mind invite heavenly images
That beckon you to have faithful visions!

Take time so "The Mind of Christ" unfolds!
As you ponder favorite Biblical promises!
You may be invited to "BEYONDER-MENTS!"
That profoundly deepens your faithfulness!
Ponder and Wonder what heaven is like
Drawing you Beyond what is after this life!

GOD'S GREAT COMMANDMENT

What does god expect from us as God's people?
What is expected of us as god's creation?
To love mercy, to do justice, and walk humbly.[56]
Loving with our whole being is god's command.

You endowed us with body, brains, spirit and mind,
Amazingly you made us in your very likeness.
What do you require of Your people, Eternal God?
Loving you with our very being is your command.

You created us with your almighty power and will,
How then should we employ these creative gifts?
May we use such gifts for our own self-interests?
We are to love neighbors with our strength.

Your love is unconditional, so how might we respond?
With all our heart, our mind, our strength and soul.
Loving enemies, our neighbors as we love ourselves?
Yes, loving enemies, friends and You, our Faithful God.

---

[56]   Micah 6: 6-8 in the <u>Old Testament of the Bible.</u>

To seek peace and justice as we try to live together.
Investing our energy, our efforts, our love and time.
Sharing hope, freedom and justice to sustain your peace,
Loving our neighbors, ourselves and our "Endless God."

GENDER ARCHETYPES IN RELIGIOUS FAITHS

In understanding faith communities, gender has relevance,
Feminine and masculine features cast shadows evidence!
This analysis examines implications of gender impact,
Upon adherents who also engage in religious practice.

Consider first the gender of the founding originators:
Buddha, Hindu, Goddesses, Jesus and Mohammed,
Plus Moses, Abraham, prophetic figures and priests.
While goddesses are noted, god archetypes persist.

In addition, make observations about faith adherents,
Predominantly, membership is composed of feminists.
Faith Communities have majorities of female members,
Obvious contrasts occur among founders and participants.

Consider key terminology that is descriptive of religions,
"The Church" is considered "Mother" with Christ as Head.
The Kingdom of God has a regal masculine connotation.
Jesus called twelve men to be his disciples for devotion.

Feminine figures are prominent in faith communities,
Mohammed's wife had a significant role in recordings.
Less is known about Buddha's attraction for feminine,
Hindu Temples reveal both male and female figures!

While there are priestesses, more dominant are priests,
   Denominational founders are masculine with exception.
Mary Baker Eddy was the founder of Christian Science,
   Many Western denominations were founded by men.

St. Peter for Roman Catholics; Martin Luther for Lutherans
   John Wesley for Methodists; John Calvin for Presbyterians.
Popes are all male with a rigid dominance of masculine,
   These examples in Christian traditions are but examples.

Why did Jesus call male disciples and women for nurturance?
   He took them away from homes and also whatever families.
He used terms like "go," "lead," "challenge" disciples,
   These are rarely terms that are applied to most females.

Feminine type concepts include "love," "believe," "faith!"
   These are predominantly feminine in contrast to masculine.
Both genders were given commensurate responsibilities,
   While women remained with children and men traveled.

Amy McPherson became a famous Evangelist in the past,
   She had a wide following as she mastered radio broadcast.
In many cultural institutions, wives have prominence.
   Illustrating these gender developments with evidence!

These gender archetypes may be subtle but are powerful,
   Most are complementarily related, but not entirely truthful.
Feminine figures are inherently more nurturing and warm,
   Masculine types adventure to explore as typical founders.

FEMININE-MASCULINE DEVELOPMENT

Both complementary and distinctiveness in development,
  From birth to maturity of genders harmonious involvement.
In fetal development, sex differentiation is already present,
  Cultural values vary about attitudes of gender preference.

Drawing upon awareness of Chinese and India cultures,
  Over-valuing male children and maltreatment of females.
Tens of millions females are either aborted or devalued!
  The Chinese policy of one-child per family was enacted.

Birth defects or accidents might be neglected if female,
  Traditionally creating problems for fostering feminine.
This has resulted in sex rations and social imbalance,
  Now for every 100 men, there are about 80 women.

Complications show up in higher level of violent males,
  Fighting for dominance plus showing domestic violence.
Addressing these problems involves changing old values,
  Plus enhancing educated girls with valuable contributions.

Education decreases birth-rate population for women,
Plus marrying later with healthier families and children!
Recent research trends already indicate these outcomes,
  Plus improvements in equality in gender relationships.

A comment by an informed Indian woman added more,
  When asked: "What are problems in Indian culture?"
Her reply: "Men! And we Mother do it!" meaning that
  Mothers spoil sons & undervalue girls making results.

In many cultures, gender development starts equal,
  Soon femininity is conditioned as well as masculine.

In childhood, boys develop aggressive behaviorally,
   While girls develop distinctive cultures of femininity.

By full gender adulthood, sexes are noticeable distinct,
   Men and women become optimally distinct in procreating.
But in later adulthood, gender patterns are reversing,
   Men become more feminine and women more aggressive.

Many men react negatively when wives go out to work,
   Men are not adapting to natural gender development.
By full maturity, male aggression reduces passively,
   While female passivity is replaced by assertiveness.

Persons resisting these natural patterns preclude
   Their own full self-development for their health.
There are even physical trends that become evident,
   Men become frailer even while women live longer.

In Jung's developmental psychology, SELF is a goal,
   SELF balances tensions of opposition of male-female.
Polarization of their persona and shadow is balanced,
   As persons naturally develop are then fully matured.

CONTEMPORARY PATTERNS

Cultures that try to counter normative gender growth,
   Compound conflicts that have negative consequences.
Many organizational institutions are slow to learn,
   Illustrations help to appreciate how to take turns.

The Roman Catholic tradition continues with masculinity.
   Protestant denominations have male and female leaders.
Over half of current seminary students are now women,
   More and more congregations have leaders as feminine.

In a role of psychological evaluations, patterns are evident,
   Ministerial candidates function more with being Feminine!
Overtly masculine characteristics encounter resistance,
   Dominated by assertiveness while lacking in sensitivity!

Feminine leadership contrasts with masculine styles,
   Overlap certainly does exist, along with distinctiveness.
Collaboration is typically practiced more by femininity,
   Competition is motivating for many of the masculinity.

Both genders exert their unique styles to be in control,
   Men tend to display control plus being authoritative.
Women subtly are more indirect in exerting control,
   Arranging schedules and pressures that come to bear.

A revealing feature involves the influence of parents,
   Many ministers have been noticeably related to Mothers.
Mothering roles are remarkably powerful in future roles.
   Fathers are also significant but are less apparent later.

In contemporary leadership, pastoral roles predominate.
   Caring-supporting-ministering to preserve organizations.
While traditional prophetic roles were mostly masculine,
   For reasons that become apparent with further analysis.

Pastor-Prophets have functions from historical patterns,
   Pastors comfort the disturbed like the sick and sufferers.
Prophets disturb comfortable to shake up establishments.
   Hostile reactions are often to stone and kill the prophets.

Religious communities are for gathering and harvesting,
   The role of hunters and explorers has notable differences.
Interesting data come from who are the missionaries,
   St. Paul, St. Peter, St. Thomas went even the farthest.

The founder of later traditions continue most patterns,
Joseph Smith aggressively led the founding of Mormons.
Hubbard is the founder of Scientology to do "clearing!"
Cult leaders are predominantly authoritative in leading.

When religious organizations counter gender maturity,
Negative consequences compound their own vitality.
Changing does not have to be revolutionary in nature,
By adjusting to natural gender growth to become mature.

Resistance to a woman for President is one illustration,
How long before a female Pope is eventually selected?
Understandably in current fixations of male dominance,
Such major developments would far into the future!

Patriarchy is one-sided control by authoritative males,
Matriarchy could also go to extremes that are opposite.
Gradual gender balance of both masculinity and femininity,
Has natural patterns of the strengths of both genders!

However, an official position in mid-twentieth century,
Declared that Mary, the Mother of Jesus was a virgin.
Plus the bodily ascension into heaven of Virgin Mary!
The Roman Catholics were affirmed by the Orthodox.

Jung had observed the imbalance in Trinitarian doctrine,
He indicated that the feminine was not given recognition.
When Mary's bodily ascension became official dogma,
He called this a Quadrinity by including the feminine.

21. GOOD NEWS: GRACE!
GRATITUDE! GLOBAL!

"Good News" is the term for Gospel!
Expressing God's Grace to His People!
This hope is designed to overcome evil!

Revealing God's Incarnation in Jesus!
Entering Time and Space as a child!
Expressing His Divine Presence!

Both Divine & human, Jesus exists!
In all the past and present He persists!
Gracious God is also eternally Present!
Sacrificing His Son in His Crucifixion!
Raised from death by Resurrecting!
Sharing Good News for all humanity!

Humanity's Hope calls for Gratitude!
Inviting people to express thanksgiving!
Acknowledging God's Gift in our living!

Appreciating forgiveness for our sinning!
Good News is designed for sharing!
To bring the Gospel to the living!

Good News is to be shared globally!
Intended worldwide with humanity!
With brothers & sisters in God's Family!

Christian communities' responsibility!
Called to share Good News globally!
Expressing Hope and Joy to humanity!

VI. MAKING POLICIES

PUBLIC and PRIVATE

Societies are guided by policies;
Whether done publicly or privately.
Policies are designed to guide practices
Civilian citizens and whole countries.

Public policies are now very important;
Guiding decisions that are significant.
Citizens need to become involved;
So that key issues are solved!

In the 1970's, I was teaching policy-making;
This was then a new field just unfolding!
I taught "Health Care Policy-making,"
"Violence, Terrorism and Peace-Making."

"A LACK OF POLICY IS ALSO A POLICY!"[57]

STEPS in POLICY RESEARCH & ANALYSIS:

Identify the Problem(s) (team is preferable)

1. List Possible Definitions. Select Best.
2. Analyze the Issues Involved:
   A. ETHICAL ISSUES
   B. FINANCIAL & POLITICAL PROBLEMS.
   C. IDENTIFY STAKEHOLDERS INVOLVED (supporters & opposition)
3. Carefully Define the Problem:
   A. TRY TO OPERATIONALIZE THE DEFINITION.

---

57   Chalklen, W., August 14, 2020.

B. REFINE DEFINITION.
(DO NOT IDENTIFY SOLUTIONS UNTIL PROBLEM IS DEFINED)
(IN MY CLASSES, THIS WAS THE 1ST HALF OF COURSE!)

4. List Possible Solutions:
   A. BE INCLUSIVE IN COVERAGE:
   B. BE COMPREHENSIVE INCLUDING ALL POSSIBILITIES you identify.
5. Prioritize Possible Solutions:
   A. RANK SO THAT BEST IS KEY SOLUTION.
6. Communicate Recommendations to Policymakers:
   (this is a key step so that stakeholders are included)
7. DESCRIBE POSSIBLE EVALUTION STEPS (including fair time in years.

WHAT JUSTICE DOES, BUT NOT DO EFFECTIVELY?

In America, we tout justice is for everyone!
Is this completely true?
When it is practiced?

There is an assumption everyone is equally protected!
But consider flagrant omission!!!
Tilted backward?

Laws are not equally enforced!
For both rich and poor!
Large corporations can violate laws repeatedly!
Enforcement of regulations varies widely
Not always consistently!

Shenanigans on Wall Street
Demonstrate unequal enforcement!
Their violations often appear to be seen as Entitlements!

Rarely do wealthy get thoroughly investigated!
Or tried for committing crimes!
Why do you think they make
Enormous contributions politically?

Poor folk receive inconsistent attention
In even minor crimes!
While poor defendants are entitled to defense lawyers
Frequently, second or third rate attorneys
Leave the poor as harvest fodder!

Advocacy for disenfranchised
Is incompetent when before Judges!
The poor cannot afford bond fees---
Then incarcerated they suffer!

Prosecutions attorneys are often
Rewarded for convictions, not justice!
Defense attorneys are overwhelmed!
Poorly prepared to present cases!

Justice differs for the wealthy----
And persons at the bottom tiers!
Others become the victims of investigations by eye-witnesses!
Until recently, "line-ups" are not accurately identified!
Under stress,
Witnesses are not reliable when feeling pressured!

Victims declared guilty!
Serve 10-25 years in prisons!
DNA testing fins gross errors
That should never have occurred!
Prosecution attorneys may withhold key defense data!
Reactive, Little Preventive

Justice reacts to violations,
But very little prevention!
Justice can try in Court
Justice can convict,
But Justice does little reconciliation!

Justice rarely prevents crimes,
Can it effect corrections?
Until wrong-doing occurs,
Justice cannot effectively stoop
transgressions!

Yes, small efforts are given to schools,
Public releases give TV vicious images
"If it bleeds, it leads" in news reports
Yes, it scares viewers!
Justice needs to be pro-active, timely and effective!

SEPARATION >ISOLATION

NATIONALISM >DIVERTSITISM

PLURALISM into GLOBALISM!

Cultures advance through stages!
For Clans and Tribes this takes ages!
The Earth is "peopled" in old cages!

Within the box of self-protection,
Outsiders are seen with suspicion!
Insiders fear Outsiders for destruction!

Inside a self-contained culture
Traditions, religions and languages!
This Isolation results in Separatism!

Walls and natural boundaries,
Protect occupants from warriors!
Until invasions break down barriers!

When resources have shortage,
Tribes search outward to forage!
Crowded areas may be invaded!

Conflicts beget more conflicts!
Violence begets more violence!
Powerful weapons may dominate!

Tribal people suspicion others,
Insiders defend against Outsiders!
Strife and war oppose Colliders!

DYNAMICS OF REFORMATIONS

Necessity prompts invention!
Pressures build up new weapons!
Battles are fought into collisions!

Winners usually dominate,
Losers are controlled and enslaved
Hatred boils over and percolates!

People have very long memories
About the treatment by enemies.
Resentments steam as unfriendly!

As warrior leaders gain powers,
Consolidating control over followers!
Authoritarian chiefs despise cowards!

Kings are honored for bravery,
They take losers into slavery!
Enslaved people keep memories!

Observation and Education do inform
How to overcome and how to reform!
Rebellion and Revolutions transform!

Our old solutions are not adequate!
Liberation & Freedom predominate!
Progressive idealism cannot wait!

Examples are French Revolutions
American, Russia, India and South Africa,
Plus North Africa, Middle East and Syria!

LIMITS OF NATIONALISM

Trade and commerce are international;
Resources and markets seek expansion!
Traditional borders preclude Globalization!

Transportation adds to transformation,
Goods and services involve communications.
Peoples exchange with vast information!

Diversified cultures have crises!
Multiple interactions and exchanges!
Breeding creative inventions as prizes!

Internet connections facilitate ideas!
Borders are unable to confine these!
Globalization complicates boundaries!

Diversity may result in pluralism,
Protective nations and tribal spasms!
Consequently, there are internal collisions!

In the century, border are strained,
The Basque and Catalans in Spain!
Scotland and England kept Great Britain!

Iraq has numerous tribal factions,
Kurds, Sunnis, Shiites and Wahabis;
Now ISIS is threatening with ambitions!

Russia is reacting to Ukraine freedom!
Putin tries to restore the Russian Empire!
Baltics and Balkans independently aspire!

Syria is torn into many vectors,
Assad holds control again warriors!
Like North Africans, tradition is sorrier!

Both India and China have problems,
Western Chinese are predominantly Muslims!
India has conflicts with Kashmir and Pakistan!

FURTURE ISSUES EMERGING

World government is widely needed
But Old Nationalism tries to prevent it!
Powerful leaders still want to be isolated!

Nuclear weapons need careful control,
   Massive destruction might come from the bold!
   Civilizations could regress to be centuries old!

Space travel could emerge in this century!
   Threats from global increases in temperature!
   How will humanity handle crises of the future?

Africa's population is rapidly expanding,
   In this century, India and China exceeding!
   Western nations are now seriously shrinking!

National borders are becoming a problem
   Global humanity calls for global citizens!
   The unknown future needs our vision!

PLAUSIBLE FUTURE TRENDS

Reflecting upon the gender specialties from the past,
   Prompts watching into the future about religious faiths.
   Trends reveal that young people are not now attracted
   To traditional institutions plus resist becoming members.

Free "spirituality" appeals predominantly for individuals,
   Joining traditional religions is less and less their preference.
   Most Protestant Churches are declining in membership,
   Inheriting one's religion from parents has less influence.

Traditions boosted by Constantine's imperial decision,
   Has given the Christian Church a dominant position.
   But that era has passed with the freedom of religion,
   Increasingly, states' major roles are clearly subsiding.

Freedom to choose emphasizes personal choice and decision,
The Sovereignty of God is the basis then for predestination.
Yes, God provides freedom of choice for each individual,
Moreover, parental influence lessens in facing freedom.

Contemporary polls recently reflect trends to be "none!"
Surveys of religious identification are "none of the above!"
Individual spirituality is among the preferred religions,
So that organizational structures have less domination.

Leadership that is characterized by nurturing hospitality,
Gives less priority to efforts for going out to evangelize.
Masculine adventurism is less prominent in priorities,
While feminine care-giving and nurturing have emphases.

Institutional patterns of religious traditions is subsiding,
Religions have fewer roles in educating and prescribing.

Contemporaries have access to communication technology,

Global communities may become connected electronically.

Cultures that facilitate full development of human SELF,
Contribute to balancing polar opposition for their health.
Rather than continuing to resist patterns of maturity,
Cultures can cultivate the genders' complementary!

"PENULTIMATES!"

Might we also recognize our human limits?
Appreciative of what we know as humans?
Accepting that we are not "The Ultimate?"
But ready to accept being "Penultimates?"

This term means "One before the Ultimate!"
Coming before the final by being resolute!
Knowing we are not the "End" but prior!
Being ready to recognize what is Earlier!

But not only Earlier but also "Eternal!"
Beyond time and space in its own realm!
These are not simple inquiries to make!
Instead raising possibilities to awake!

ISMS, SCHISMS AND MORPHISMS

Human history has excesses and obsessions!
Arguments and war are fought with brains and possessions!
Unfortunately, innocent lives are lost to unneeded aggressions!

When favorite theories become challenged,
Our parochialism dominates those who are offended,
Duals, debates and battles break out as bloody fights started!

In the previous verses, both known but also hidden,
Notorious struggles are satirized that are often forbidden,
Do not expect enlightenment, humor or conflicts for schisms!

Change calls for both flexibility and also adaptions,
As human beings, we will have many new options!
To move on ahead "Beyond to Emerging Horizons!"

FINALE

In this decade we have changes;
New global leadership is here!
We hope for an upward swing;
From "Meism" to sing "Weism!"

Individualism leaves our others;
Humans are sisters and brothers!
Together we make a new start,
Sharing Religions, Sciences and Arts!

Inequalities result in many fatalities,
Economically we have casualties.
We hope to work more together
So that all citizens live better!

With concern for persons everywhere
We all can contribute here and there!
So our future will hopefully improve;
While expressing our Winsome Love!

YES, OUR WORLD IS CHANGING! TOGETHER WE ARE SWINGING UPWARD!

"Be the change you want to see in the world!"

Mahatma Gandhi[58]

---

[58] The Author was invited to teach at Colleges of Mahatma Gandhi University.

BIBLIOGRAPHY

Acton, Lord, 1952 The Collected Works of Lord Acton.

Ahsani, Syed and Basheer Ahmed, 2008, The Golden Age of Islam.

Aung San Suu Kyi,

Chalklen, W., August 14, 2020.

Cristakis, Nicholaus A., April 30, 2012, "Hans Rosling: Poet of Percentages as Statistician," Newsweek.

cummings, e.e. playwright of "It Should Happen to a Dog!"

Einstein, A., 1917, Cosmological Consideration in the General Theory of Relativity, Berlin.

Figes, O., 2012, Just Send Me Words: A True Story of Love & Survival in the Gulag, Metropolitan Press.

Frank, Evolutionary Economics, Cornell University Press.

Frankl, V., Man's Search for Meaning.

Gugenbuhl-Craig, A.,

Hayward, P, "Naked Pastor."

Holy Bible, New Testament, First Corinthians 13.

Long, Joshua, Jan-Feb. 2013 "Awakening" in The Atlantic.

Kepler, J., 1596, Mysterium Cosmology.

Khater, S., "The Rich are Different; they are Ruthless!"

Krugman, P., 2020, ARGUING with ZOMBIES, W.W. Norton & Company, New York.

Melville, H., Moby Dick.

Middents, G., 1967, The Relationship of Creativity and Amxiety, Ph.D. Dissertation, U. of Minnesota. Mpls.MN.

Ibid., 2007, BRIDGING FEAR and PEACE: Manipal University Press.

Ibid., 2018, Personal Meaning DeMystified, iUniverse Press, Wilington, Ind.

Ibid., 2019, CREATIVE BEYONDERING, McNaughton Press,

Ibid., 2019, HEATING the EARTH: GLOBAL WARMING, iUniverse Books.

Lev M. and Svetlana I. Just Send Me Word: A True Story of Love & Survival in the Gulag!

Long, J., Jan.-Feb., 2013, "Awakening," The Atlantic.

McLaren B., 2019, God Unbound.

Melville., H., 1851, "Moby Dick,"

Middents, Gregory, 2014, JAIL DIVERSION, Masters Degree Thesis, University of Dener.

Millar G., 2007, THE CREATIVITY MAN: an Authorized Biography, Scholastic Testing Service, Inc.

Mishchenko, L. and Svetlana Ivanova

NASA National Air and Space Administration.

Niebuhr, Reinhold, 1939, The Nature and Destiny of Man.

Piaget, J., The Psychology of Genetic Epistemology.

Piketty, T. 2020 CAPITAL and IDEOLOGY, Bellnap Press of Harvard University Press.

Price, Margaret "Ultraflex Jobs: You Coose Hours and Venues," The Christian Science Monitor, July 4, 2011

Principles of Rotary International.

Putnam., R., 2020, THE UPSWING, Simon and Schuster, New York.

Rosling, H., 2019, Ten Reasons We Are Wrong About the World and Why Things are Better Than You Think,

Flatiron Books.

Sau suu Kyi, Aung, "One woman's inner strength," July 11, 2011, The Christian Science Monitor

Semuels, A., February 3, 2020, "Finding a Changing World," TIME.

Sheldon, A.F. 1911, Principles of Rotary International, "Rotary's Two Official Mottoes.

Smith, A., 1776, The Wealth of Nations,

Sultan, E., Loyalty: The Vestine Virtue.

The Bible, Old & New Testaments, Oxford University Press.

Weaver, E., : What I Learned After I Knew It All!

Wells, Samuel, April 17, 2013, "Forgiving Ahab: Naboth's Vineyard and God's Justice," Christian Century.

Whedbee, J.W., 2002, The Bible and the Comic Vision, Minneapolis: Fortress Press.

Wilkerson, I.S. 2020, CASTES: The Origins of Our Discontents, Random House, New York.

Wilson, E.O., 2012, The Social Conquest of the Earth!, W.W. Norton and Company, Ltd.

AUTHOR'S BIOGRAPHY

Gerald "Jerry" Middents' has wide experiences after serving as a US Air Force Captain. He became a Presbyterian Minister and earned a Ph.D. He served as a Professor of Psychology at Austin College.

Invitations to teach at Universities in India, China, Poland and Slovenia. He taught at Mahatma Gandhi U. primarily at Union Christian College. Then he filled the Endowed UNESCO Peace Chair at Manipal University. Lecture invitations came from University of Texas at Dallas, Ljubljana U., Mangalore U., St. Paul's College, five medical schools, six seminaries and several community colleges.

His poetry books include Personal Meaning DeMystified; Heating the Earth: GLOBAL WARMING; Earthlings and Spacelings, SPORTS and RELIGIONS TOGETHER. He published other books, journal articles, sermons and lectures. Creativity, Policy-Making, Peace and Justice are his specialities.

Printed in the United States
By Bookmasters